COURAGE IN THE CLASSROOM

LGBT TEACHERS
SHARE THEIR STORIES

EDITED BY CATHERINE LEE

JOHN CATT

First published 2020

by John Catt Educational Ltd,
15 Riduna Park, Station Road,
Melton, Woodbridge IP12 1QT

Tel: +44 (0) 1394 389850
Fax: +44 (0) 1394 386893
Email: enquiries@johncatt.com
Website: www.johncatt.com

ISBN: 978 1 912906 96 3

Set and designed by John Catt Educational Limited

Dedication

To all the LGBT teachers that proudly went before us. We stand on the shoulders of giants and know that our lives as teachers are better, and this book is only possible, because of your courage.

Acknowledgements

Thank you very much to all the teachers who have contributed to this book. It has been an absolute privilege to get to know and share your stories.

Catherine Lee

Contents

What is 'Courageous Leaders'?

Courageous Leaders is an LGBT teacher leadership programme financed by the UK Department for Education's Equality and Diversity fund. It provides mentoring, training and support for LGBT aspiring school leaders over a 12 month period, with the aim of helping them achieve promotion as their authentic selves. Workshops promote confidence building, develop the communication and presentation skills of participants, and examine what it means to be LGBT and an authentic school leader. Courageous Leaders are recruited through word of mouth, via flyers distributed at London Pride celebrations and via LGBT social media networks.

About the editor

Dr Catherine Lee is deputy dean for education at Anglia Ruskin University in the East of England. Catherine works with teachers, school leaders and students to promote diversity and inclusion in education and is a passionate advocate of authentic leadership. She has published extensively on the theme of LGBT teachers in schools and her articles have attracted national media interest. In 2019, Catherine was named as one of the top 100 LGBT people in the UK in *The Independent's* Pride Power List. Catherine is a mentor and one of the strategic leaders of the Courageous Leaders programme. She is also on the board of trustees at The Kite Trust, a charity supporting LGBT young people and their families.

The contributors

JESSE ASHMAN

Jesse Ashman has previously worked as a youth worker, mental health recovery worker and community development coordinator. He currently works for The Outside Project (the UK's first LGBTIQ+ crisis/homeless shelter) and as an account manager for a workplace inclusion programme. He also has a master's degree in sexual dissidence from the University of Sussex and a black cat called Bruce, whom he loves dearly.

JEROME CARGILL

Jerome is new to teaching in London, having spent most of his ten years teaching in New Zealand. He is a media and film studies specialist, and has also been a head of year and professional development leader. In London he is now teaching at William Morris Sixth Form in Hammersmith. In New Zealand, Jerome was a leader in developing schools' inclusive cultures and supporting LGBTI+ students. He was a member of the Post Primary Teachers' Association Rainbow Taskforce, which involved delivering a 'safer schools' programme in various schools around the country. He was also an executive adviser on the board of the youth organisation InsideOUT, who work to give rainbow people in Aotearoa New Zealand a sense of safety and belonging in their schools and communities through various projects. Jerome intends on making the most of his UK visa by learning from the UK education system and adding many new stamps to his passport.

SARAH CARROLL

Sarah Carroll is a teacher of health and social care at a sixth-form college in Cambridge and has been teaching for eight years. She completed her undergraduate degree at Coventry University and her PGCE at Newman University in Birmingham.

CERIAN CRASKE

Cerian Craske is a second-year English student at Cambridge University. She was part of the group who founded the Nonsuch High School for Girls LGBT+ society with Catherine Halliwell.

CATHERINE HALLIWELL

Catherine Halliwell is a mentor on the Courageous Leaders programme. She is currently head of science at Nonsuch High School for Girls, after teaching in London state schools for 18 years. Catherine is also a school mental health champion and has set up an LGBT+ society for students.

DEREK MANSON

Originally from rural Canada, Derek Manson works at a primary school in Newham in London, where he is a Year 1 teacher and the art and design technology subject lead. Derek is also the National Education Union representative for his school and a member of the school wellbeing team. In his spare time, Derek enjoys pursuing new interests, trying exciting new activities and going on travelling adventures.

YVONNE MARSDEN

Yvonne Marsden (a pseudonym) entered the teaching profession in the early 1980s. She taught in two comprehensive schools and two independent schools during her 35 year career, enjoying senior leadership roles in three different schools. Yvonne has a master's degree in leadership and professional development, studied during a year's career break. She is still actively involved in education as a governor, researcher and consultant.

JOHNpAUL McCABE

Johnpaul McCabe is a teacher of modern studies at Prestwick Academy in Scotland. After studying politics and social policy at Stirling University and the University of Illinois, Johnpaul worked in the Scottish charity sector before completing a postgraduate diploma in education at Aberdeen University.

NIAMH McNABB

Niamh McNabb is head of studies at Long Road Sixth Form College in Cambridge, where she manages guidance staff, is part of the safeguarding team, and is equality and diversity lead. Long Road is a large sixth form offering A levels and diplomas to almost 2300 16- to 19-year-olds. Niamh has worked in education since 1999, following on from her career in photography and magazine journalism. Before that she graduated from the University of Nottingham with a physics degree, and is one of the few teachers who has taught extensively across the arts and sciences. Her passion lies in pastoral work; she has been part of Long Road's senior guidance team since 2011 and head of studies since 2014. Niamh was in the first cohort of Courageous Leaders and is now a member of the strategic leadership team.

JANE ROBINSON

Jane Robinson is the founder of the Courageous Leaders programme. She began teaching in 1987, and taught English and Drama in secondary schools in inner London. She eventually had the courage to come out to her colleagues, in 1990, and then to pupils and parents in 1998. Jane moved to Newham local authority in 2003 to become an advisory teacher; here she encountered an open working environment where she felt for the first time that she could be herself in the workplace. Jane returned to teaching in 2010, this time in primary schools. Although some of the primary-school communities were traditional and conservative, Jane felt comfortable to speak to parents about her wife and children and didn't face any negativity. In 2015, Jane moved to the HEARTS Academy Trust in Essex. This multi-academy trust is a place which actively supports diversity and Jane immediately felt at home. It was here with the support of her school leadership colleagues that she founded Courageous Leaders.

JILL SOUTHART

Jill Southart is a retired assistant head (student wellbeing) at Nonsuch High School for Girls, where she works with Catherine Halliwell.

DONNA WALSH

Donna is a member of the Courageous Leaders strategic leadership team, and director of the Teaching School for BMAT Education – a multi-academy trust based across Essex and East London. She is also a specialist leader of education with a focus on initial teacher training. Donna completed a master's degree in education leadership in 2015 with a focus on middle and senior leadership training. Donna is an alumni facilitator for Ambition Institute, and also facilitates the National Professional Qualification for Middle Leadership (NPQML) and Senior Leadership (NPQSL) at the Institute of Education in London.

HANNAH WICKENS

Hannah is head of department for PSHE at Monega Primary School and a Year 6 class teacher. An avid musical theatre fan and travel lover, this will be her fourth year of teaching.

Defining key terms

Throughout this book you will see contributors refer to sexual and gender identities in a number of ways. Some have opted for LGBT (lesbian, gay, bisexual and transgender). Others have added an I and/or a Q for intersex and queer respectively. One or two teachers have described their identity as queer: a non-normative expression of gender and sexuality favoured by those who reject labels.

At Courageous Leaders, we believe that it is vital that teachers can be themselves. Consequently in editing this book, I have resisted any urge to provide a consistent approach to the naming of sexual and gender identities. These identities belong to the teachers who have told their stories. I hope you enjoy reading them and that you are left feeling inspired.

Catherine Lee

Introduction
Catherine Lee

I feel extremely privileged to be able to share this collection of stories from teachers who came together through the Courageous Leaders programme, the UK's only leadership development programme for LGBT teachers. Each LGBT teacher has written about what in education is most important to them, and all the stories are very personal. Some work in primary schools, some in secondary education. Some are in the state sector and others work in independent schools. One or two have now left teaching. They are based in towns, villages and cities across the UK, and one or two reflect on life overseas. Some teachers present a historical perspective and celebrate how things have changed for the better in schools. Others talk about the importance of safe spaces for LGBT teachers, of being roles models for young people, and of individual struggles to find out and assert who they really are. For some teachers, these accounts have been extraordinarily painful to write. For others they have been cathartic, or empowering. For most, this is the first time they have told their story and certainly the first time it has appeared in a book. In every case, the stories of our Courageous Leaders hold important learning for school leaders, governors, policy-makers, colleagues, parents and students.

The book starts with my description of the climate for LGBT teachers in the UK. Jane Robinson, the founder of Courageous Leaders, next shares the steps she took to set up the UK's only LGBT leadership programme. Then over the course of 14 chapters, the Courageous Leaders tell their stories. Some recall teaching in the 1980s and 1990s under Section 28 (which prohibited the promotion of homosexuality in schools), and some examine their experience of teaching in schools in 2020. Each LGBT teacher concludes their story with a piece of practical advice for school leaders, teachers and governors keen to make their schools as inclusive as possible for their LGBT staff.

In the first of our stories Catherine Halliwell, a Courageous Leader participant, and most recently a mentor on the programme, reflects on her own leadership journey and her commitment to supporting the mental health of her students. To add a further dimension to her own account, she has invited an ex-pupil to write from her perspective about the LGBT club they asked Catherine to set up. Then, one of Catherine's senior leadership team contributes her viewpoint on the important work that Catherine has done in their school.

We are all a product of the times we have lived through and for some of us, Section 28 left a deep-seated legacy which to this day means we guard our privacy fiercely. In chapter two, Yvonne Marsden (a pseudonym) compares her experiences as a lesbian teacher in the state and independent school sectors during the years of Section 28, reflecting on the way in which despite the homophobia of the era, Yvonne's colleagues offered her support when she lost her long-term partner to a terminal illness and at other times of great personal challenge.

Jerome Cargill began his teaching career in his native New Zealand. In chapter 3, in the first of three contributions from Jerome, he compares his upbringing and early teaching career in New Zealand with his more recent role as a teacher in London. Throughout his story, he reflects on the importance of good communication and a strong sense of community in helping LGBT teachers to become their authentic selves in the school workplace.

In chapter 4, Hannah Wickens – a lesbian teacher relatively new to the profession – reflects on her initial anxieties about working with Muslim colleagues she wrongly assumed would reject her same-sex relationship. Hannah also explores how since coming out, she has been empowered to set up an anti-bullying campaign for pupils at her school, and discusses the positive impact this has had.

In chapter 5, Niamh McNabb, in a powerful and moving story, explores her gender and sexuality histories (her 'double whammy').

She reflects on the challenges she faced in becoming her authentic self and, crucially, the way in which her school supported her at times of considerable challenge.

In chapter 6, I describe an incident that led me to leave teaching for good after more than 20 years in the profession. After a homophobic neighbour and parent of children at my school exposed my sexual identity as part of a malicious allegation, I learned the extent to which, in my rural school community at least, parent power was more compelling than any right to protection from discrimination.

Derek Manson is a teacher in East London. However, he was born and raised in rural Canada. In chapter 7 he describes some of the challenges he faced as a pupil in a small, traditional and conservative school community. He then explores the ways in which his own experiences as a pupil have shaped him as a teacher. In particular he examines his commitment to inclusion and his determination that no child will ever suffer as he did at school.

In chapter 8, Sarah Carroll – a teacher in Cambridgeshire and a mentor on the Courageous Leaders programme – shares her story. Sarah examines how she navigated the intersection of her professional and private selves, particularly in the school staffroom, and finally found the courage to come out at school. Sarah concludes by reminding us of the responsibility we have to our students to be our authentic selves and to celebrate diversity.

Donna Walsh is one of the leaders of the Courageous Leaders programme. As a heterosexual and cisgender ally, in chapter 9 she explores her own upbringing in Ireland and examines her own role and contribution to the Courageous Leaders programme.

Jerome Cargill returns in chapter 10 to consider his experience as a leader of continuing professional development for teachers in New Zealand. As part of the National Teachers' Association, Jerome led the Rainbow Taskforce, working with teachers to encourage greater LGBT inclusion in New Zealand's schools. In this chapter, Jerome reflects on some of the challenges of trying to affect positive change as an outsider to the schools he worked with, while acknowledging the fear of change and his own fear as a queer visitor to each of the schools.

Jesse Ashman is not a teacher, but in chapter 11 he presents a very candid and thought-provoking analysis of schools. As a self-described queer and gender non-conforming youth leader and trainer of leaders, he explores authority and the power structures that exist within schools, and what it means to subvert this authority. Making uncomfortable reading for some, Jesse argues that our effectiveness as school leaders should be judged on our ability to nurture young people to be self-reflective, critical thinkers that are able to express themselves in the most honest and authentic way possible. Jesse says that although Section 28 doesn't exist anymore, heteronormativity and cisnormativity are still alive and well in our schools.

In his final contribution to our book, Jerome Cargill presents in chapter 12 a short but thought-provoking vignette based on his experiences as a solo traveller. Jerome considers what it means to be an outsider in a new country and reflects on what this can teach us about creating schools and classrooms that are welcoming and truly inclusive, and which allow our students to be their authentic selves.

In chapter 13, we meet Johnpaul McCabe, a teacher of modern studies in Scotland and someone who travelled further than most to join the Courageous Leaders programme. Johnpaul looks at the inclusion of LGBT teachers within school communities. Starting with a reflection of his own upbringing and the challenges he faced as a pupil at school, Johnpaul recommends some principles for schools that can help to create inclusive and safe spaces for all LGBT stakeholders. Throughout his narrative, Johnpaul argues that when schools get inclusion right for one diverse group, they get it right for everybody.

It seems fitting that the final story from our teachers comes from Jane Robinson, the founder of Courageous Leaders. In chapter 14, Jane describes the challenges she faced as a teacher during Section 28 and reflects on the ways in which teaching is now a much more welcoming profession for those teachers identifying as LGBT.

Finally, I bring the book to a close by revisiting the Courageous Leaders programme and, drawing on the testimonies of our Courageous Leaders alumni, examine the way in which the programme has impacted those who have participated. This is followed by some suggestions for what you might do in your own school to create a safe and welcoming workplace for your LGBT teachers, LGBT pupils and LGBT families.

The UK climate for LGBT teachers

According to the UK government's *LGBT Action Plan (2018): Improving the Lives of Lesbian, Gay, Bisexual and Transgender People,* acceptance of same-sex relationships among the general public is at a record high and continues to increase, with 64% of the UK public saying that same-sex relationships were 'not wrong at all' in 2016, up from 47% in 2012, and 11% in 1987. Despite this, the survey showed that many LGBT people do not feel comfortable being themselves in the UK, and no more so than in the workplace. Of the 108,000 LGBT people surveyed by the government, almost a quarter had experienced a negative or mixed reaction from others at work, due to being (or perceived as being) LGBT.

There is evidence to suggest that schools are particularly challenging environments for LGBT teachers. Despite legislative protection, recent literature about LGBT teachers continues to record concerns about discrimination in UK schools. Evidence suggests that many LGBT teachers do not yet feel adequately protected in schools. There is an enduring climate of fear about coming out in the school workplace, and one in four LGBT teachers believe that their LGBT identity has been, or is, a barrier to promotion (Lee, 2019a).

LGBT diversity in school leadership in the UK has suffered through a persistent culture of moral panic related to LGBT identities and the education of children. In 1988 in the UK, the Conservative government under Margaret Thatcher was responsible for the implementation of Section 28 of the Local Government Act, which stated that:

A local authority shall not– (a) intentionally promote homosexuality or publish material with the intention of promoting homosexuality; (b) promote the teaching in any maintained school of the acceptability of homosexuality as a pretended family relationship. (Great Britain. Local Government Act, 1988)

Although Section 28 referred only to local authorities, the common belief at the time was that schools under local authority jurisdiction were indirectly bound by the same rules. Though the Section 28 legislation was never enforced, in the 15 years between 1988 and its repeal in 2003, many LGBT teachers feared the loss of their jobs if their sexual identity was revealed.

Since the repeal of Section 28 in 2003, several pieces of legislation have helped to give LGBT teachers occupational security in the UK. The 2003 Employment Equality (Sexual Orientation) Regulations and Part 3 of the 2006 Equality Act gave all employees the right to be protected from homophobic bullying, and prevented any employer from discriminating against or harassing workers on the grounds of their actual or perceived sexual orientation. The 2010 Equality Act categorised sexual and gender identity as protected characteristics that are free from workplace discrimination. However, while anti-discrimination policies are symbolically important in school communities, LGBT teachers report that equality policies have not enhanced their feelings of personal or professional security, nor have they made them any more willing to disclose their sexual orientation to either their colleagues or students (Lee, 2019b).

In 2019, the Conservatives, under Prime Minister Theresa May, to some extent atoned for their Section 28 bill by legislating that from 2020, compulsory relationships and sex education (RSE) in schools would include recognition of same-sex couples and families for the first time. While this was broadly welcomed by teaching and LGBT communities, some parents and faith communities were vehemently against the new ruling, claiming it was counter to religious teachings, particularly Islam and Catholicism. The RSE guidelines state that parents may not withdraw their children from health and relationships education. They can withdraw their children from sex education (a request that secondary-school headteachers can only deny in exceptional circumstances), although once students reach the age of 15, they can override their parents' wishes and attend sex education lessons even if their parents do not approve.

Government ministers in 2019 were accused of mounting a State takeover of parenting, and a parliamentary petition signed by over 110,000 people called on the government to give parents the right to opt their children out of RSE entirely.

In May 2019, parents held a rally outside parliament during the time the RSE guidance was being debated, calling for the full right of withdrawal from RSE lessons to be awarded to parents. Protests took place outside schools too, beginning in Birmingham, where the openly gay teacher Andrew Moffatt had introduced a No Outsiders programme some four years earlier. No Outsiders is a charity that has produced children's books depicting some characters with same-sex parents. Protests quickly spread to other schools using the No Outsiders resources, notably in Manchester, Bradford, Northamptonshire and Kent.

Headteachers and teachers in schools have called for urgent support from the government amid fears that the disruption could escalate further. Section 28 left a legacy of caution and anxiety for the LGBT teachers who experienced it, and many of these teachers now draw parallels between Section 28 and the RSE controversy. Despite equalities legislation protecting LGBT employees, the lived experiences of many LGBT teachers suggests that schools are not yet places where LGBT teachers are able to be their authentic selves.

Setting up Courageous Leaders
Jane Robinson

In 2014, the government provided a modest amount of funding to support equality and diversity in the education workforce. Based on the protected characteristics in the 2010 Education Act, teaching school alliances were invited to bid for funding to support teachers who were either women, from a black or ethnic minority, disabled or LGBT+. The aim was to encourage people from diverse backgrounds into positions of school leadership. The initial project in 2014 was a huge success and established initiatives such as WomenEd and BAMEed. However, no one applied for funding for LGBT+ teachers.

In 2016, encouraged by my headteacher, I began the process of applying for funding with the aim of setting up a leadership programme for LGBT+ teachers. I was asked to provide data on the numbers of LGBT+ teachers and the rate at which they achieved promotion. I contacted every teaching union to be told, much as I expected, that such data was not collected. I submitted the form without the data required and to my surprise and delight secured the funding anyway.

Now came the difficult part: where was I going to find 15 LGBT+ teachers who were seeking promotion? I knew of two gay men who worked in my multi-academy trust but I had no idea if they would be willing to participate in the programme. They turned out to be thrilled at the prospect and one of them said he knew the perfect mentor who he was sure would be interested in being involved. The other said he was sure one of his colleagues was bisexual and he'd ask her when he got the chance. I had three of my fifteen and made the decision that, as it was a leadership programme, not all the mentors had to be LGBT+, they just had to be leaders.

As a teaching school director I attend regular meetings in my locality. I created a leaflet advertising my programme and took it along to these meetings. I had never discussed my sexuality with other teaching school directors; it just wasn't a subject that came up. I tentatively offered my leaflet and felt my face redden as I asked the other directors to find out if they had any LGBT+ teachers who wanted to participate in my new programme. There was an awkward silence and then someone laughed. 'How on earth can we do that? We can't ask people if they're gay, can we?' Then one of the directors came to my rescue and said, 'I'm pretty sure I can find you two people.' He did just that and I doubled my cohort.

I'm a governor in a school in East London so I asked if I could distribute my leaflet there too. I found three more people: a lesbian, a gay man and a bisexual woman. I advertised through the National Education Union and recruited a gay male teacher from Pontefract.

September 2015 arrived and we were due to launch the Courageous Leaders programme later that term. I found out a colleague lived with his male partner and so approached him about joining the programme. He agreed and I had my first cohort. I now needed to convey the values that underpinned my programme. I reflected on these for several days, canvassing the views of colleagues and friends. I decided on promoting inclusion, celebrating diversity, accepting difference, challenging the status quo, and achieving social justice.

I wanted the participants to be ready for promotion and to have the skills that required, but crucially to feel confident as LGBT+ people. I had a mix of primary and secondary teachers, all at different stages in their career and all with differing opinions on whether they should be 'out' as teachers. I wanted to support their promotion aspirations and also give my programme a uniquely LGBT+ flavour. We opened our first face-to-face day with an inspirational speech from a gay headteacher, then worked in groups on leadership traits, assigned mentor time and invited the participants to share their own stories.

The evaluations made it clear that the most valuable part of the session was anything that allowed the participants to discuss their sexual and/or gender identity and how it impacted on their school life. I had found quite a few LGBT+ mentors and the participants revelled in the opportunity to discuss their promotion plans with someone who really understood what it was like to be both a teacher and LGBT+. I also discovered that the mentors loved their new roles and many of them went over and above the mentoring plan, keeping in touch with their mentees very frequently. To my relief, participants and mentors all returned for our second face-to-face day. One of the mentors shared her harrowing experiences as a teacher in a conservative rural community (see chapter 5), which participants described as moving and inspirational.

On our final face-to-face day I drafted in support from the company Craft of Communication, who specialised in techniques for interview and presentation skills. One of the London mentors agreed to hold the day in her school in order to keep the costs down and I began to realise how incredibly supportive and generous everyone was being.

At the end of the year all but one of our Courageous Leaders had gained promotion. Three had become heads of school, while others had become lead practitioner, assistant head, SENCO (special needs coordinator) and lead for equality and diversity. We had successfully completed our first year and all I had to do now was find another 15 LGBT+ teachers who were ready for promotion! The difference was that this time I wasn't on my own and I now knew exactly what the participants wanted. Our Courageous Leaders certainly did want promotion and they wanted support to acquire the skills to achieve that but, more importantly, they wanted a safe space to discuss their vulnerabilities, with colleagues who understood exactly how they felt about their sexuality and its impact on their career.

So how does it work? More about the Courageous Leaders programme
Catherine Lee

In this final part of the introduction, I examine in more detail the effectiveness of our Courageous Leaders programme and its benefits for participants. Drawing on the evaluation forms and written testimonies of some of our participants, I try to capture the motivations of participants for joining our programme and their experiences during the face-to-face days. Where I have quoted participants, pseudonyms have been used to anonymise their contributions.

In order to access the programme, the participants have to seek the permission of their headteacher to release them from school for three face-to-face days, with the Courageous Leaders programme paying for teaching cover. Each of the participants is then at least open to their headteacher about their sexual/gender identity prior to embarking on the programme. The face-to-face training days largely take place in London at a variety of venues, including a university, a primary school and a teachers' training centre. The London base has inevitably led to the majority of participants being based in London or the South East, but we have also attracted participants from as far away as Bristol, Yorkshire and Ayrshire.

The face-to-face sessions are spread throughout the year and cover a range of themes and activities, broadly categorised as follows:

- Leadership styles.
- Verbal and non-verbal communication skills.
- LGBT leaders sharing their experiences.
- One-to-one mentoring.
- Networking.

Our Courageous Leaders commonly identify a number of challenges in being an LGBT teacher and aspiring leader, and describe how these motivate them to participate in the programme. Anxiety in the workplace and being wary around school stakeholders is a common theme. LGBT teachers recognise the importance of moving between schools to gain promotion, but concerns around navigating personal and professional identities and in particular 'coming out' in each new job cause considerable apprehension, and dominate participants' thoughts when contemplating applying for promotion. The risk of moving schools and either being discriminated against or not being able to come out makes participants wary, and adds a layer of complexity to career decision-making. Where LGBT teachers move to new schools for promotion, anxiety is initially high. Andrew, a gay male teacher with five years' experience, moved schools to be a head of music but initially regretted the decision.

'I wanted to … see if I was able to be the leader I believed I could be, but in the early days of my latest job I struggled a lot with anxiety and was afraid I had made the wrong choice in moving.' (Andrew)

Courageous Leaders speak regularly of feeling isolated in their current roles, and engage with the programme because they do not know any other LGBT people in their schools. Kwane, a gay male secondary-school teacher of politics who had only recently started teaching, said:

'As a gay man new to the profession it can at times feel a bit isolating and [I] hoped to benefit from meeting others and learning from their experience to help me overcome my internalised fears and anxieties.' (Kwane)

Feeling 'othered' and consequently vulnerable in the school community is something a number of Courageous Leaders talk of struggling to overcome. Many are ambitious but lack the confidence to put themselves into roles where they are more visible within the school community, as this comment from Andrew articulates:

'I was excited to attend a programme specifically for LGBT teachers, as I had never previously had an opportunity to be out at work, and this was something I felt strongly about. I particularly felt vulnerable in a new leadership position and was nervous about exposing my true self. I was excited to share and listen to other [LGBT teachers'] experiences ... as I did not know any LGBT teachers who were in any sort of school leadership role.' (Andrew)

This comment captures the value of LGBT-specific leadership training, not least for networking. The absence of visible LGBT leader role models can deter LGBT teachers from putting themselves forward for senior leadership positions, perpetuating schools as sites of heteronormativity (presumed heterosexuality), and leadership as, visibly at least, only heterosexual.

Many LGBT teachers are motivated to join the Courageous Leaders programme because they want specific guidance on whether or not to disclose their sexual or gender identities at school, fearing that it may adversely affect opportunities for promotion. There is particular concern about whether or not to disclose their sexual identity to students, fearing what colleagues and particularly the parents of pupils will think. Clare, a lesbian primary-school teacher with 18 years' experience, aptly captures her concerns and motivation for joining Courageous Leaders:

'I was excited to attend a programme specifically for LGBT teachers, as I feel sexuality brings with it fear and uncertainty, particularly thinking about whether or not to come out at school and the adverse effect this could have on my career progression.' (Clare)

LGBT identities are often fused with unhelpful discourses of hyper-sexuality, with same-sex sexual identity being imbued with notions of sexual acts in the way that heterosexuality is not. When applied to teachers, LGBT sexual identity is too often conflated with child protection discourses, due in part to the tabloid press historically associating male paedophilia (with boys) with homosexuality. When concern is expressed about the influence on young people of openly lesbian or gay teachers, schools are perhaps instead trying to protect the conservative and heteronormative status quo. Unfortunately, when every child is a potential victim of sexual abuse, every teacher becomes by default a potential perpetrator.

Overwhelmingly, the major reason cited by participants for wanting to join the Courageous Leaders programme is the absence of any other sort of specific LGBT support network for teachers, as Clare described:

'There isn't a support network in teaching for LGBT people and I hoped this programme would offer that. It can be so isolating when you are not out to anyone at school.' (Clare)

Workplace friendships and networks are key to fitting into existing work cultures and developing managerial and leadership identities. However, LGBT teachers often avoid contact with one another within the workplace for fear of being outed through their associations with one another. It is important then, as Andrew, Kwane and Clare identified, that a safe professional network of LGBT support is available outside the workspace. Courageous Leaders meets this need for the LGBT teacher participants by providing a safe space in which common concerns and experiences can be shared and solutions developed.

The Courageous Leaders programme consists of three face-to-face days spread throughout a single academic year, with email, telephone and social media support available between each of the face-to-face days. On the face-to-face days, the same cohort of 10 to 15 LGBT teachers meet together, accompanied by their LGBT leadership mentors. The mentors are all in leadership roles in education, either in schools, initial teacher training or universities.

The sense of an LGBT community for aspiring leaders is recognised by all participants as a strength of the programme, as Helen, an experienced head of physics in a secondary school, states:

The sense of an LGBT community was nurtured quickly in the group. This provided a safe, trusting and insightful view of leadership, especially addressing LGBT issues in schools or our own personal challenges. Previously I felt much more isolated and now I do feel as if I am part of a larger community, facilitating change and support for LGBT students and staff. The course has had a huge impact on me in this field.' (Helen)

It is clear that the participants value feeling part of a community in a way some of them had struggled to do in their schools. Spending time as their authentic selves within the sort of community they lack in the workplace develops their confidence, allaying fears and anxieties about the dissonance between their professional and personal identities, as Eve, a lesbian primary-school teacher with over a decade's experience, describes:

'The size of the community that is out there to call on for support made a strong impression on me and I realised that so long as the right culture is created in school, there should be no reason why anybody should be worried about talking about these issues in school.' (Eve)

Over the course of the year-long programme, Courageous Leaders is frequently referred to by participants as their 'safe space'; a place where they can let down their guard and not worry about managing the intersection of their professional and personal identities. Several express that this is a relief, allowing for a greater focus on leadership without worrying about identity management. Ben, a secondary-school teacher relatively new to teaching, describes the clarity of focus and thought he gained once the issue of sexual identity was no longer apparent:

'[It] allowed for frank, open and stimulating discussion in a safe environment where we could discuss challenges faced and be solution-focused. This was incredibly empowering where I could be an open and out professional without the hesitation or afterthought of what my colleagues may think of me. This enabled me to feel more confident and able to actively participate without the hesitation that so often influences my decision-making process in new situations.' (Ben)

Ben's reflection hints at the way in which managing his sexual identity erodes his confidence in the school workplace, by causing him to be wary and hesitant in his interactions with others.

The Courageous Leaders do not only gain support from their mentors; there is a sense of mutual support through the sharing of common experiences, as Clare explains:

'Hearing from other people about their experiences as an LGBT teacher showed me that some fears I had were shared. It also meant we could lean on each other and provide advice where needed.' (Clare)

The programme helps participants become more at ease with themselves, and helps them reconcile their LGBT and teacher identities so they can focus on developing leadership skills. Fraser, an ambitious gay man in a middle leadership role, captures this:

'Through the training provided, I feel I am more self-confident and I feel more settled and accepting of my LGBT status within the teaching profession .... Hearing about the experiences of others has made me feel much less alone in my school journey. Furthermore, it is because of this course that I feel less apprehensive about hiding my personal life.' (Fraser)

The way in which the Courageous Leaders programme reduces anxiety and facilitates self-acceptance within a safe space is recognised as impacting positively on mental health, as Helen acknowledges:

'It should not be underestimated, the positive effect of support for the LGBT individual on their mental health and overall wellbeing.' (Helen)

The value of the Courageous Leaders programme as a resource for LGBT teacher wellbeing and good mental health is echoed by two further participants who admitted to bouts of debilitating depression. A sense of harmony with one's environment is one basis for good mental health, and when there is disharmony between the individual and the dominant culture, the resultant stress is significant. It is evident that during their face-to-face days, the Courageous Leaders value the 'time off' from their dissonance with their school environment, as well as the chance to be in a professionally stimulating environment without the burden of managing the intersection of their personal and professional identities.

During the programme, the LGBT teachers participate in a workshop on communication and presentation skills, led by a facilitator from the Royal Academy of Dramatic Art. Participants are given coaching to develop their own leadership attributes, focusing on creating a positive first impression, effective and appropriate non-verbal communication, and confident public speaking. Most Courageous Leaders note an absence of LGBT leader role models in their schools, and for some this means they are unsure how to embody leadership authentically. The Courageous Leaders programme works with individuals in the presence of the entire cohort, co-constructing what it means to be a school leader while being their authentic selves. This session is overwhelmingly rated as the most rewarding and highly valued aspect of the programme. The comments below are typical of several:

'I personally enjoyed the training we were provided regarding presentations and speaking to a large audience. This practical hands-on training is something I use in my own practice now.' (Fraser)

'The day with the communication facilitator was a highlight. I am quite shy and although passionate when I speak, I can forget to breathe! The skills I learned in the session I am slowly taking on board, and I used them when I presented at a national event this week.' (Helen)

The practical activities in which presentation and communication skills are practised and coached in front of others appear to sit at odds with the tendency of LGBT teachers to try to remain as invisible as possible in the workplace. Grace, a PE teacher with ten years' teaching experience, found that:

'The most valuable moment was when we were taught presentation skills by a theatre company. I legitimately hated every second of it as I was very much outside of my comfort zone, but I have learned a great deal about how I come across and [have] grown as a result of it.' (Grace)

As school leadership in the UK remains overwhelmingly male, heterosexual and masculine, the visible lack of confidence among the participants may be attributed to insecurities around their suitability as a leader. During the programme, some of the mentors lead whole-group workshops in which they share their experiences of navigating their heteronormative school communities and achieving their leadership roles in spite of their LGBT identities. The speakers are described as inspirational role models by several of the participants. Helen, a secondary-school head of science with 12 years' experience as a teacher, valued hearing from an openly gay male headteacher:

'I didn't think it would be possible to be a headteacher and be out at school. But I know now that it can be done and this has renewed my ambition to be a head all over again.' (Helen)

Helen's lack of access to LGBT leadership role models had caused her to give up her ambition of becoming a headteacher, but hearing from a gay senior leader, out to his staff, pupils all other school stakeholders, motivated Helen to resume the quest for leadership that she had abandoned because of her sexual identity.

During each of the face-to-face days, participants meet with their mentors one to one, to plan and work together towards the leadership aspirations identified at the start of the programme by each participant. In between the face-to-face days, mentors keep in contact with participants via email or phone, advising and supporting them prior to making applications for promotion by reading over personal statements and CVs, and later offering interview preparation, or rebuilding confidence where participants are unsuccessful. After 21 years in the same school, Isabel gained the confidence by working with her mentor to successfully apply for a head of school in alternative provision. Isabel clearly appreciated how the mentorship developed her confidence:

'My mentor supported me to do the relevant research, and the coaching and mentoring and interview practice helped me to apply for the post. In the past I hadn't had the confidence to look elsewhere for a job. I felt safer staying put.' (Isabel)

With the help of her mentor, Grace was also successful in becoming a head of year; a promotion that took her out of a role she had been in for more than six years. Grace wrote:

'I was recently granted a promotion in my current school which would have been difficult to etch out without the help of my mentor. They have been contactable at the touch of a button and often offered insights that I would not have been able to access otherwise.' (Grace)

Andrew likewise achieved promotion to head of music and attributed the support from his mentor to being instrumental in helping him maintain his confidence through the application and interview process:

'I found the contact with more experienced mentors to be invaluable. I found it so useful to reach out for support from my mentor, they spurred me on when I was doubting myself and was convinced I wouldn't get the job.' (Andrew)

Developing and co-constructing authentic models of leadership is a key component of the Courageous Leaders programme, underpinning all of the face-to-face days. Authentic leadership can be described as self-awareness of an emerging process where one continually comes to understand his or her unique talents, strengths, sense of purpose, core values, beliefs and desires. Authentic leadership relies on relational transparency; authentic leaders value open and honest communication and relationships with those they work with. In one cohort, two participants reported that as result of the programme, they applied for and secured leadership roles they would not have felt capable of applying for without this guidance and the confidence to be their authentic selves. Joanne, a sixth-form science teacher for 10 years, describes how the programme spurred her on to achieve promotion to head of sixth form within a multi-academy trust:

My mentor provided me with the confidence to be myself and take my whole self to work. With this increased confidence, I was motivated to apply for a promotion I thought was beyond me. This is just the beginning, as a result of working with my mentor, I will definitely apply for further senior leadership roles in future.' (Joanne)

Joanne's reflection implies that the sense of relief in finding her authentic self and a way to embody leadership authentically helped her to succeed in gaining promotion. After 21 years at the same school, Isabel too notes that it was through finding her authentic self as a potential leader that she gained the confidence to apply for promotion elsewhere. She wrote:

'The programme gave me the confidence to be myself as a leader, and I applied for promotion as head of alternative provision. I start my new role in January.' (Isabel)

It is clear from the testimonies of Courageous Leaders participants that once they permit their personal and professional identities to coexist, their confidence as potential leaders grows. With the help of their LGBT mentors, they are motivated to realise goals that had in some cases been abandoned due to the perceived complexity of managing their personal identity within the context of being more visible through their leadership role.

Having explained what our Courageous Leaders programme is all about, it is now the turn of the Courageous Leaders themselves to share their stories.

REFERENCES

Great Britain (1988) *Local Government Act 1988*. London: The Stationary Office.

Lee, C. (2019a) 'Fifteen years on: the legacy of Section 28 for LGBT+ teachers in English schools', *Sex Education* 8 (1) pp. 1–16.

Lee, C. (2019b) 'How do lesbian, gay and bisexual teachers experience UK rural school communities?', *Social Sciences* 8 (9) pp. 249–258.

1: Becoming an LGBTQI+ leader and supporting student mental health
Catherine Halliwell

In this chapter, Catherine reflects on her own leadership journey and her commitment to supporting the mental health of her students. She has invited an ex-pupil to write from her own perspective, and one of Catherine's senior leadership team has also contributed her viewpoint on the work that Catherine has done.

I start this emotional reflection with a school report. Not any old report pulled out from under my teenage bed, but my current school's 2017 Ofsted report:

> The school fosters good relations and celebrates differences between pupils, for example through the work of the lesbian, gay, bisexual and transgender group. (Ofsted, 2017)

I must admit, my own school experience was never reflected so well in an Ofsted report. Certainly not in my Northern comprehensive in the 1980s, when Section 28 gagged our teachers and the alarmist AIDs campaigns curtailed our adventures.

Once I advanced to sixth form, it was the house music scene and the newly launched C4 TV channel that led me to recognise and celebrate the diversity of life – of gender, sexuality, ethnicity and faith. But as I progressed through a local university as an undergraduate and postgraduate, I still kept my personal life secret. Questions of my needs and desires I did not need to sidestep, as they were never discussed. The heteronormative culture of the UK prevailed with strength and dispassionate legislation.

A fortuitous move to London guided me into the 2000s, as I began living with a truly diverse group of international people. We were an eclectic assortment, from acrobats and academics to therapists, theatre directors and archivists. We found commonality through food, language and the proud acceptance of our diversity.

It was from this cauldron that an opportunity to train as a teacher emerged. I had realised that the stress of the closet, the constant walking between two lives, the double-checking, half-lies, secret crushes and trying to find my path in life, while hiding behind a variety of addictions, had all taken their toll. The inevitable burn-out, helplessness and anxiety that this led to caused me to reflect, come out to my parents, get counselling and develop my inner calm. I had changed my life and now would change my career.

In short, I started the journey to become a leader – both in the classroom and within the more formal school structure. Initially I used my subject-specific 'nerdery' to support my students to develop academic outcomes. However, I quickly realised I needed to reach further, as compassion and an understanding of the complex needs of my students was crucial to success in the classroom. A distinct understanding of emotional intelligence was required; I needed the language of emotions that had evaded my childhood. I learned new skills and realised my wellbeing needed to improve. Emotional intelligence helped me to monitor and identify emotions. Then I used that information to guide my teaching and path through life.

My first teaching role was at a hugely diverse, mixed comprehensive, with a powerful, compassionate and highly effective senior leadership team. These were my first role models; my guides to building my confidence as an openly gay science teacher. There are so many stories I cannot share in a professional manner, but needless to say we were a tight-knit collection of staff, working tirelessly to give our students the advantages in life that most folk take for granted.

I grew professionally to be honest, trusting, appreciative, cheerful and proud to be a teacher. Many out teachers populated the school, but beyond the staffroom the picture was different. Personalised support for individual students was the prevailing culture. The general approach was for inclusion and support, but to the detriment of LGBTQI+ specific advocacy and leadership.

Nearly a decade later, I challenged myself to teach in an academic girls' grammar school. The energy was different, the students and parents were still demanding, but the perspective had changed. Again, there was a range of gender and sexual identities among both students and staff. Once again, LGBTQI+ advocacy and leadership were hidden. A formal and visible LGBTQI+ strategy and culture were only just developing in schools across the country.

Perhaps unexpectedly, it was Ofsted who helped to facilitate positive change when they highlighted actions to prevent homophobic and transphobic bullying in their inspection criteria (Ofsted, 2013). Backed up by the 2010 Equality Act, discussions were catalysed in senior leadership teams across the country. The work of teaching unions, the Department for Education (led by the openly gay education secretary Justine Greening), and many agencies – including high-profile campaigns by Stonewall, the LGBTQI+ lobbying group –helped to command a more open LGBTQI+ culture in schools. The support, safety and confidence of LGBTQI+ students and staff in our schools were at last brought to the foreground.

So when in 2016 a member of the senior leadership team warned me of an email that would arrive shortly, from a group of students who wanted help setting up an LGBTQI+ society in school, the timing was wonderful. I laughed and asked 'why me?', but really I was touched that they had been brave, reached out and trusted me. I had not yet realised, but my life became a little bit brighter that day.

The email duly arrived: 'Dear Ms Halliwell. We'd like to set up an LGBTQI+ society in school. Can you help please?'

They'd taken a risk. They did not want to assume I was gay, but they did know they needed some help. I did not realise at this stage that I also needed some support. Not just to set up the LGBTQI+ society, but to armour myself with further skills that would come from a wide range of sources.

We decided to meet weekly at lunchtime, initially with 20 students (and hundreds of sweets). Another teacher kindly volunteered to be present too. This was the start of the visible support for the LGBTQI+ community in our school.

As a lifelong learner, I knew that training would be important. I met with our senior leadership team for guidance and suggested a Stonewall 'Train the trainer' course, which they promptly signed off. Here I met staff from across the UK who were passionate about building LGBTQI+ inclusive strategies and guiding each other on how to navigate the sometimes overwhelmingly negative experiences in their schools.

As our LGBTQI+ society grew in numbers, so did our enthusiasm. We had bake sales, developed PSHE resources, trained allies, celebrated LGBTQI+ History Month and led whole-school assemblies.

Over time our self-assurance also grew. We now have an annual pride week that coincides with sports day (lots of opportunities for flags), an open evening (perfect for conversations with prospective parents) and the school birthday. We coordinated with the history department to produce a school-wide activity linking riots and rights, to demonstrate that civil disobedience and rights are the foundation of our society (remembering the 50th anniversary of the Stonewall riots). We've developed INSET for all staff and are currently organising a film festival.

Following a volunteering role for London Pride, I learned of a new training opportunity: Courageous Leaders. This course offered a timely opportunity to develop my confidence as an out LGBTQI+ staff member and demonstrate the leadership skills required to take my career further. It was exciting to work in an exclusively LGBTQI+ environment where we could share our unique experiences, both personal and professional. Effective communication, mindfulness, Myers–Briggs personality tests, mentoring and coaching were used to encourage us to understand and be our authentic LGBTQI+ selves, to take a lead and to apply for promotions.

The unique aspect of the course was the sense of LGBTQI+ community that was nurtured in the group. This provided a safe, trusting and insightful view of leadership, especially when addressing LGBTQI+ issues in our schools. The course meant I certainly felt much more confident in my professional life as an out LGBTQI+ member of the school community. I now had a backup team. I was able to articulate and communicate with greater effect, both personally and in a larger forum. The course had a huge personal impact – for the first time I felt like I belonged. The positive effect of support for the LGBTQI+ individual on their mental health and overall wellbeing should not be underestimated. I had a new perspective; I no longer had a poor opinion of myself.

Thankfully, mental health is becoming openly discussed in classrooms. Despite many years of neglect, teachers are now finding the tools to sign-post students to guidance. In 2018, I took up an offer of 'Mental Health Champions' training from the charity Place2Be, specifically addressing emotional wellbeing, attachment theory, solution-focused techniques and working with parents and carers. Through my own journey as a nerdy gay woman, I had become aware of the challenges to mental health while developing in a heteronormative culture: the internal homophobia, lack of representation, alienation and lack of role models, coupled with little guidance on how to live your best gay life, how to live authentically and how to have a child in a gay relationship – all this guidance and more I needed. My teenage years watching LGBTQI+ TV movies had not covered any of these situations!

As an out LGBTQI+ leader I could now discuss all of these issues with staff and students. I could advocate for alternative families and inclusive PSHE sex education. I could try to make sure that examples of LGBTQI+ individuals are confidently discussed when they are in our syllabuses (Isaac Newton, Francis Bacon, Pyotr Tchaikovsky, Jackie Kay, Sally Ride and Hatshepsut), that gender-neutral language exists in our school reports, and that all student identities are all proudly celebrated in our community.

I've been fortunate to have been supported to encourage our LGBTQI+ society to take on new challenges, to respond to their needs and to represent both staff and students. I'm now confident in delivering INSET to all staff, sharing with them the language that challenges heteronormative generalities and empowering them to be the wise, sensitive professionals that they aspire to be. I've been able to advise SLT on our trans protocol and to take a lead in embedding policies and facilitating cultural change, while developing my own leadership skills.

I'm fortunate that in my 20-year teaching career I have been blessed with thoughtful and progressive headteachers, who have been responsive to change and supportive in their actions. Conversations have always been positive, and these headteachers have been brave in challenging homophobia or transphobia in their schools. Certainly I have been backed up. I've been impressed by their support, which has allowed me to be my visible and authentic self in school and to discuss this in the classroom, staffroom or office. Having these conversations can make such a difference, and it is a privilege to support young people by providing a safe place to express their sexuality or gender.

I'm a little proud that I've become the role model I would have wanted at school – the teacher that could tell me it's ok to be different and demonstrate a path through life as a happy, successful and independent gay woman. The teacher who I knew I could approach, who would be happy to advocate for a wide range of students. Someone who supports positive mental health, coordinates school policies, celebrates pride week, shares our inclusion on open days, decorates the school with flags and posters, and most importantly can safely be themselves at both home and work. Such an approach is now being modelled for all groups in school as, for example, discussions on neurodiversity develop.

The confidence I've gained as an out LGBTQI+ leader should not be underestimated. After four years as an out LGBTQI+ leader, I'm now mentoring other LGBTQI+ staff on their journey towards becoming leaders. Furthermore, those initial students who emailed me about setting up an LGBTQI+ society have gone on to take student leadership roles in the school, develop their own societies in further or higher education, speak out at national events, be recognised with Jack Petchey awards, contribute their LGBTQI+ school journey to academic books and even produce LGBTQI+ theatre. For most of my life I've felt an outsider, but now that I have a place, I'm optimistic, proud, peaceful and excited for the rest of the journey. I feel courageous and thanks to my peers and students, I am my authentic self. Surely that only reflects beautifully on them.

My story is really a story of confidence and teamwork that illustrates how small intentional steps can lead, over time, to a cultural shift that supports the LGBTQI+ community in our schools. A positive approach to change is often slow, and it is the collective effect of many small actions that makes a difference to the self-esteem of the whole school community.

Coming out is an ongoing journey with no end. It has involved the slow reveal to myself, friends, family and colleagues, but also the daily challenging of the heteronormative assumptions in schools and wider society. Having the confidence and language to share our stories is a way to challenge the prevailing culture. Visibility in schools really does matter to create safe spaces for us all.

A student's view
Cerian Craske

When we first sent off the email to Ms Halliwell that would lead to the formation of the LGBTQI+ society, there was one main concern on our minds – did we guess wrong? We didn't want to have wrongly assumed that a teacher was gay (even though we'd said nothing of the sort in the email, just asked for help). Despite this, all of us – young, newly out at school as LGBTQI+ and trying to find our place in the world – had known from the start that Ms Halliwell would be the best person to turn to. As it turned out, we were right, and that email was the start of something which would permanently change my experience of the school.

The LGBTQI+ society started small. We took over one of the school IT rooms once a week, brought skittles and smarties, and tried to educate people about our experiences and provide a safe space for other LGBTQI+ students. It had never been hard for people to tell that I was gay (to this day, the only family members I've 'officially' come out to are my parents; the rest guessed long before I had to tell them), but at that point I was still nervous, still trying to figure out what my identity actually meant for the rest of my life. LGBTQI+ narratives did, and still do, overwhelmingly focus on teenagers and on the process of coming out itself, so once I felt like I'd completed that particular chapter, I had no idea what I was supposed to do next. No one teaches you how to exist as a gay person (not that anyone teaches you how to exist in general, I suppose), and I found it hard to project what my life would look like; a struggle which I'm sure is familiar to other LGBTQI+ people. Having a visibly LGBTQI+ teacher combatted this, as for the first time there was someone older than me who wasn't just another student, who had a life and friends and a job, and I found it a little less hard to visualise myself as a gay adult.

The society changed over the years. The initial committee that set it up was made up of three couples, and since we were all 15 this dissolved fairly quickly, leaving other people to take the reins. I no longer needed the group in quite the same way over the next year or two, but I found myself going back and speaking to the younger students, trying to show them the same potential for the future that I'd felt. One of the greatest moments was our 'big gay bake sale', in which we filled the school hall with rainbows and sugar and blasted gay anthems over the sound system, and sold out of cakes within minutes. Admittedly, it's easier to get people to support you if you give them cake, but it still felt pretty good to know that everyone knew we were gay and proud and was happy to give us their support.

After I left school, I came back in to help out with pride week. To stand up in front of teachers I'd known for years and students I'd never met before was such an incredibly empowering experience, which I never would have had if Ms Halliwell hadn't responded favourably to that email years ago. I also brought in Ray Harvey-Amer, local LGBTQI+ activist and one of my family friends, who was astonished at the sheer amount of LGBTQI+ visibility in the school. I didn't know how to respond to this, because I was surprised as well, as even in the short time I'd been at school attitudes had changed so much.

I'm in my second year at university now. I've been as involved as pos-sible in the LGBTQI+ community, with LGBTQI+ open mic nights and pride events forming a significant part of my timetable. I'll admit that when I went back to school recently to run a workshop, running into Ms Halliwell and letting her know that I'm still 'living my best gay life' felt great. I've definitely grown up a long way from the nervous 15-year-old who sent off that email, and it's been amazing to see how the school has changed even in the short time since I left, with far more LGBTQI+ visibility than my younger self could ever have dreamed of.

LGBTQI+ in schools: an SLT perspective
Jill Southart

This summer I retired from teaching after 35 years, the last ten of which were as a member of the senior leadership team in a large all-girls grammar school, with responsibility for pastoral care and wellbeing support across the school. To say that the visibility of the LGBTQI+ community in the school changed during that period would be an understatement; what follows is a personal perspective on that journey.

Shortly after taking over responsibility for pastoral care in the school in 2009, I was approached by a small number of students saying that they would like to set up an LGBTQI+ society. (This was actually the first iteration of the society; Cerian's account above describes the second version.) There was no overt culture of homophobia in the school, but LGBTQI+ issues had never been particularly high on anyone's agenda. I certainly had no objections to the idea and took it to the senior leadership team for approval. Concerns were raised: would parents object? Could we be seen to be promoting a particular 'lifestyle'? In the end, it was decided that the society could run, but with certain caveats in place: it would have to be closely monitored by a member of staff (as with all clubs and societies), and only students in Year 10 and above would be allowed to attend.

The society ran with a smallish membership (20 or so) for a couple of years and no one, either in or outside the school, raised any objections. The profile of the group remained relatively low-key: they would meet on a weekly basis to discuss issues of their choice and, most importantly, support each other in discussing their own personal issues. When the particular group of sixth-form students who had started the group left at the end of Year 13, no other students wanted to take on running the group and it fell into abeyance.

Over the next few years there was therefore no LGBTQI+ society in the school, but the need for one was becoming much more obvious, in conjunction with the increased need for pastoral support in general. Much has been written and debated about the perceived rise in mental health issues among young people over the past few years, and the arguments are now very familiar. Several factors are thought to be contributing to this rise, such as increased pressures at school and in society as a whole, combined with the increased prevalence of social media and cyberbullying. It is also the case, of course, that greater awareness and less stigma surrounding mental health issues has encouraged more young people to come forward and talk about their problems. Whatever the truth behind the increase, the practical impact in schools is plain to see: an apparent rise in anxiety, depression and mental health issues, sadly resulting in increased self-harm and hospital admissions among young people.

It is not of course true to say that being LGBTQI+ means you will automatically face mental health issues, but it certainly seems to make that possibility more likely. Stonewall's *Prescription for Change* report found that lesbian and bisexual women had higher rates of suicidal thoughts and self-harm compared to women in general (Hunt and Fish, 2008), and it has been shown that of all the common sexual identity groups, bisexual people most frequently have mental health problems, including depression, anxiety, self-harm and suicidality (Nodin et al., 2015).

Certainly, our experience in school began increasingly to reflect these findings, as young LGBTQI+ people seeking support began to articulate more clearly their concerns around their sexuality. Often those concerns centred on the fear of how their parents would react. The conversation would usually begin around a non-specific mental health issue – perhaps anxiety or low self-esteem – but with encouragement, students began to talk more freely about their worries and we were able to signpost them to appropriate support groups. We would reassure them that we would not be contacting their parents, but encouraged them to talk to their parents themselves when they felt ready; those who did so were invariably surprised to find that their parents were supportive.

It was clearly necessary for us to increase our more formal support for LGBTQI+ students in the school, and over time this is exactly what happened, as we became more aware of the issues faced and more adept at responding to them. In-house school counselling services were rapidly developed, often filling the gap in the external support provided by services such as CAMHS, which were struggling to cope with increased demand. Greater emphasis was placed on LGBTQI+ issues in the PSHEE curriculum and in assemblies, and staff training focused on how we could better reflect LGBTQI+ issues in our own subject curriculums.

Just as importantly, the LGBTQI+ society was resurrected in 2015 under the leadership of a new group of keen students (including Cerian) and guided by Catherine Halliwell, who overcame her own reticence to talk about such a personal topic and thus became a superb role model for all students in the school. There were no longer constraints about what could be discussed or the age of students who could attend. The society rapidly grew in membership, support and activities, and it soon had more than 60 regular members, some who identified as LGBTQI+, some who were questioning and some who were allies. As a result, the profile of the LGBTQI+ community in the school has risen exponentially. The testimonies offered by Catherine and Cerian give a flavour of the work that has been done. There are now posters around the school; staff wear rainbow lanyards; and as the school's open evening coincided with pride week, hundreds of prospective students and their parents were welcomed to the school at a reception festooned with LGBTQI+ displays, which occasioned some interesting conversations!

Perhaps one of the most important lessons we have learned at the school is recognising that we don't always get it right straightaway. Some years ago, when we had our first openly transgender student in school, we struggled with the practicalities: what name should we be using on official documents such as exam certificates, which toilets should he use, and so on. There were also legal implications – our admissions policy admits only girls, and our uniform code required all students to wear a skirt. But with lots of support from the young person's parents, the charity GIRES and the school's lawyers, we were able to offer a comfortable and inclusive environment at a challenging time of transition for this student.

A measure of the school's success was that when it was time to opt for sixth-form study, he did not choose to leave and attend a mixed college, where integration might have seemed potentially easier, but instead remained at our school where he felt supported and included. Since this time we have had other students who are at varying stages along their own journey, such as some who want to be known by a different name or by male pronouns, for example; we still make mistakes but it is fair to say that we now feel more confident in offering the right support.

It is, of course, extremely difficult to quantify the impact which these developments have had on the wellbeing of individuals, but from my experience working in this field I am in no doubt whatsoever that the current atmosphere of inclusion in the school has led to improvements in the mental health of many students. Teenagers (and adults) who are questioning their sexuality face many challenges, not least of which is acknowledging their identity to their parents, and I have seen all too often the mental health difficulties this can cause. We are not at the end of the journey, and there is always more work to be done, but without a doubt the vibrant LGBTQI+ society and the ethos of inclusion in the school as a whole provides these young people with a safe space in which to be themselves.

Advice for an LGBTQI+ inclusive school from Catherine Halliwell

It is the accumulation of small intentional steps that lead, over time, to a cultural shift that supports the LGBTQI+ community in our schools.

REFERENCES

Hunt, R. and Fish, J. (2008) *Prescription for change: lesbian and bisexual women's health check 2008.* London: Stonewall.

Nodin, N., Peel, E., Tyler, A. and Rivers, I. (2015) *The RaRE research report: LGB&T mental health – risk and resilience explored.* London: PACE.

Ofsted (2013) *Exploring the school's actions to prevent and tackle homophobic and transphobic bullying.* Manchester: Ofsted.

Ofsted (2017) *Short inspection of Nonsuch High School for Girls,* https://files.api.ofsted. gov.uk/v1/file/2653701. Manchester: Ofsted.

2: A tale of two settings
Yvonne Marsden

In this chapter, Yvonne Marsden (a pseudonym) compares her experiences as a lesbian teacher in the state and independent school sectors during Section 28, reflecting on the way in which her colleagues offered her support at times of great personal challenge.

Early life and education

I am a 'baby boomer', born at our home in a village in East Anglia. My parents were manual workers who had left school in their early teens, and although we had little in material terms, my brother and I were surrounded by loving family, friends and neighbours. Growing up in the countryside we enjoyed the freedom and happiness of a relatively simple life. I attended a small village primary school, where a dedicated headmistress took an interest in me, offering me opportunities to extend and reinforce my learning. The potential she saw in me was realised when I passed my eleven-plus and qualified for entry into a girls' grammar school in the nearest town.

Looking back, my grammar school education was to define many aspects of my future self – it introduced me to sport, science and my first love! Growing up in the village, I was blissfully unaware of people other than the heterosexuals surrounding me. This was a time without gay role models in the positive way we see them today, with the most memorable gay character on TV (and the only one I can recall) being the comedic Mr Humphries in *Are You Being Served?*. Far from being accepted, my perception was that being gay was the subject of ridicule.

I thrived at secondary school, stimulated by a rigorous, classical education and enjoying the sporting opportunities on offer six days a week. In some ways it was not easy though; it was over an hour's journey each way and none of my school friends were local. This resulted in a strong sense of dislocation – I was in many ways unlike the predominantly middle-class pupils at school, but I was also increasingly unlike my family. In her book *School Wars*, Melissa Benn (2012, p.144) claims that 'private schools perpetuate segregation and inequality, divide neighbourhoods, friends and even families'; something in my experience that could also be claimed about grammar schools. My dislocation was brought home to me emphatically by my brother, who warned me that I was 'in danger of becoming a snotty middle-class kid who doesn't fit here'. Although it hurt at the time, his words hit home and helped me to balance my two lives better after that.

My sport-filled teenage years saw me enjoy relationships with boys and think no more about it. Until, that is, I fell for one of my friends; I realised that I felt differently about her, an attraction more powerful than I had felt for my boyfriends. Life had begun.

After sixth form, I became the first from my family to go to university. Although I initially found being away from home difficult, I loved the whole experience – sport, sport, sport, punctuated by a great music scene and enough study to respectably survive. While I enjoyed a great social life, and struck up close friendships with men and women, I did not have any relationships during that time. After my first degree, I stayed on to complete a PGCE and so began my career as a teacher.

State school life in the country

My first teaching appointment was at a comprehensive based in a small town. My time there was enjoyable but not particularly noteworthy. The pupils offered me enough challenge to learn how to discipline effectively, my colleagues were friendly, supportive and encouraging, and it gave me a solid start to my career. I was ambitious, though, and two years into my career I started looking for promotion.

Throughout my teaching career I have also pursued my love of sport, first as a player and then as an official and administrator, and it was through this that I met Mary. A few years my senior, Mary worked in industry and had previously only been in heterosexual relationships, including a marriage which had ended several years before we met. Mary and I were close friends whose relationship evolved into something long-lasting and very special.

Early on in our relationship I secured my first promotion, to 'teacher in charge of subject' in a small, rural secondary school. Glade Secondary School was a former secondary modern, with only a few hundred pupils on roll and underwhelming public examination results. What it did have, though, was a senior team determined to give pupils the best possible experience, and this resonated strongly with my own philosophy. This was an exhilarating time in my career in many ways, as the teachers at Glade were dedicated, hard-working and highly skilled. We saw public examination results improve dramatically and numbers on roll soar. My first management role saw me essentially being in charge of myself, as the only teacher of my subject, but I soon found myself managing the department.

Glade was in a small town, with a wide catchment of rural primary schools. Throughout my time at the school, in common with many of the participants in Catherine Lee's (2019b) study of LGBT teachers in rural schools, I lived outside the catchment area. Reflecting on her own findings, and those of others, Lee (2019a, p.680) found that teachers do this to 'create a safe space and actively protect themselves against public scrutiny or interest in their personal lives', and I think this was true for me. I was in a relationship with Mary, but I was not out at school. I didn't ever make up a male partner, but I think I lived my life in more of a 'don't ask, don't tell' way. I was a confident teacher, and a confident person, but I knew that I didn't want to bump into pupils or parents outside school. When I say I wasn't out at school, I also don't believe I was in denial. Mary was always welcome at school and our relationship, although never articulated, was accepted, or at least tolerated. She attended events if she wanted to and was always invited.

In the staffroom, I believe my persona was professional, caring and friendly. Members of my department might also have described me as driven and a bit fiery – I don't think I've ever lacked courage as a leader, but it would be fair to say that at that time I was predominantly an instructional leader. In the classroom, I was firm but fair, and while friendly towards the pupils, I was very work-focused, never inviting any questions of a personal nature. Whatever the pupils may have thought of my private life, they never asked about it. Nor was I subject to the sort of taunts or bullying that I know some gay teachers experienced. When Section 28 was introduced in the late 1980s, I had already been at Glade a few years and was quite well established, but nevertheless I felt its impact. I clearly remember experiencing the 'fear of loss of employment' that Gill Clarke (1996, p.191) found in her study of lesbian PE teachers in the 1990s. Mary and I had discussed the situation and I was adamant that I would never deny our relationship; if asked, we agreed that I would acknowledge it, even if that meant losing my job. It was a very scary time. (Writing that here really brings home to me how terrible this whole situation was!)

I found the Glade community unerringly supportive, and it was here that I started my leadership journey. I rose from teacher in charge of subject through to head of science, and then five years after joining the school I was appointed deputy head. I think it helped that I lived the life of Anna Marie Smith's (1994, p.205) 'good homosexual', though, not the 'dangerous queer'! My behaviour was never threatening or what others might perceive as inappropriate. Sexuality was not something openly discussed at that time, but I remember a wonderful senior teacher called John initiating a conversation with me one day about sexuality being a spectrum, not a simple binary, long before this came to be an accepted reality. I always enjoyed working with John and knew that if my Section 28 nightmare became reality, he would take care of me.

Having been the only gay (that I knew of) in the school community, when we appointed Sam as an NQT in the PE department, I suspected that I was no longer alone. She fitted in perfectly at the school and was an outstanding teacher. Socially, though, life in the town was far quieter than she was used to. Well-meaning colleagues frequently asked her if she had 'a nice boyfriend', and despite her unerring patience and good humour, she eventually snapped. At the staff Christmas meal, when asked this question once again, she emphatically told them she had not got, and never would have, a boyfriend, but she did have a very nice girlfriend! When a sheepish Sam called me to tell me what she'd done, we laughed and laughed. In some ways I envied her – she came out because she wanted to, but my outing was not so positive; I came out through need.

After a relatively short period of being unwell, Mary underwent blood tests and was diagnosed as being terminally ill. Our world fell apart. I carried on working, but I was a mess and it showed. After repeated questions, I gathered my closest colleagues around me and told them the situation. I needed them and they were there for me. This was long before the repeal of Section 28 and although I'm sure people already had their suspicions, they now knew that I was gay. I remember very clearly one friend, a devout Catholic, finding me later that day to say, 'I believe your life is lived in sin, but you are my friend and I love you, if there's anything I can do please just let me know.' Whatever their personal convictions, this summed up very well how colleagues approached me over the months to come.

Mary and I enjoyed a stable, loving relationship for over 15 years. We were devoted to one another and would certainly have married had that been an option in those days. Sadly, Mary passed away within months of her diagnosis. I then felt the full force of Glade community love; colleagues and governors offered their support, and even the odd parent learned what had happened and offered their sympathy.

By the time I left, I had been teaching at Glade longer than I had lived with my parents. The school and its community had nurtured and supported me; it had allowed me to develop as a teacher and taught me how to manage people effectively, with courage and clear direction, mixed with empathy and a personal interest in each individual in my care. They believed in me and taught me to believe in myself. I had promised Mary that I would not rush into moving after she had gone, but my heart was no longer in my work and I decided to take a year out.

Independent school life in the city

Writing this account has made me reflect on what I did in the next phase of my life, perhaps for the first time in depth. Looking back, things all happened a bit too quickly. I fell hook, line and sinker for Becca, a young, successful city dweller; when she showed interest in me I was flattered. Before my feet had touched the ground I was seeing her and had decided to relocate; I was moving to the city. Becca was very comfortable being a lesbian, she was out at work and had a strong circle of gay friends. My new life was to be very different.

Having been a deputy head, I started applying for management posts in state schools in the city. I knew these schools would be very different to Glade, but I was determined to continue my career in the maintained sector. Sadly, this was not to be. Whether schools thought 18 years in one school was too long, or my skills and qualities were not what they were looking for, I don't know, but I did not get as much as an interview.

Fate then led me to apply for a head of science post at Fairland College, an independent school where some of my sporting friends worked. They knew the post was coming up and encouraged me to apply. It was an independent school – definitely not something I would have considered if I had not been getting desperate. My application was successful and I resumed my career on the other side of 'the great divide'. Much to my surprise, I loved it. The pupils were attentive and hard-working, with a city edge that kept them interesting. Some members of staff were much more old-school than I was used to, but they were professional and welcoming. It was also extremely gay-friendly; I went from being one of two at Glade, to one of around twenty at Fairland.

As a gay woman, teaching at Fairland was liberating. The school staff were inclusive and gay-friendly; it was easy to be comfortable with my sexuality in this setting. I was out with staff, but as at Glade, never with pupils. There were undoubtedly pupils who knew, such as those with parents on the staff, but I have never been a teacher who shares her private life with her pupils. As a teacher of science, this has always been my focus; pupils in my lessons concentrate on learning. That's not to say my lessons were very formal; as a scientist there were lots of times, such as when pupils were doing practical work, when we could chat more informally, but that tended to be about sport or news stories.

When I moved to Fairland, I thought my days in senior management were behind me; middle management would suit me just as well. I had underestimated, though, how difficult I would find it not to have as much influence over whole-school issues as I had been used to, and within a few years I had been promoted to an assistant headship. My life experiences and leadership evolution made me a far more reflective manager this time around – more consultative and collegial – and I enjoyed my work life. Becca and I regularly attended events together, and she was fully integrated into school life. While positive in very many ways, this was ultimately to be difficult for me, as our relationship did not last.

When I discovered that Becca had been having an affair with one of our friends for several months, I was devastated. As our relationship ended, my self-confidence and sense of self-worth plummeted, and my mental health suffered. This was exacerbated by teaching in an environment where I was surrounded by mutual friends. I was so lost that a young teacher who I worked with in science recommended counselling; a move that I honestly think saved me. So a year after our break-up, I started to love myself again and it helped me to see that I needed to change my situation. I started looking for a new job.

I also started to do things again, including taking myself to concerts, shows and even away for weekends. It was on one of these weekends away that I caught up with an old friend who I knew from our sporting days. Seeing Frances again was to change my life! We had always been friends, but here we were two decades later, both single, both somewhat damaged from previous experiences, and slowly but surely, we fell in love.

As my fortunes turned, much to my surprise I was called for interview at The Elysian School, one of the top schools in the same city. Elysian was another independent school, but with a reputation for being considerably less liberal than Fairland. When I was invited back for a second-round interview, I wondered if my sexuality would be an issue in this new post, so I called my head to see what he thought. He assured me that it would not be a problem, because 'the head knows you're gay, I told him you're in a stable relationship'. While I was relieved to hear this, Frankie was furious as she felt they should not have been having this discussion. Of course, she was right, but I headed into the next interview secure in the knowledge that only my ability would matter.

I secured the job and joined Elysian as deputy head. This was the first time I had reached the senior leadership team externally, and after the previous few years I knew it was a courageous move, but I also instinctively thought it would be a positive one. I think at this point I returned to my authentic self, both in terms of my senior leadership role and, more importantly, my relationship. Elysian was an extremely high-achieving, hard-working school where I was judged solely on my ability to do my job. My open, honest approach to staff led them to trust me and seek my help. In return, I had some of the wisest minds I have ever worked with around me, resulting in deep collegiality and shared leadership. Frankie and I were invited to school events and sometimes she came, sometimes she didn't, just as the partners of other senior leaders did. She was always welcome and always introduced as my partner.

The Elysian School was an incredible place to work, where I was stimulated and stretched by my post, and thoroughly enjoyed my teaching; although no longer 'young', the ambitious, driven me was back with a vengeance! One of the things I liked about my time at Elysian was that colleagues, and especially the head, frequently drew on my state-school experience, particularly areas such as using data and teaching and learning strategies. We also worked alongside local maintained schools on projects, which I really enjoyed as it allowed me to draw on skills I had developed throughout my career.

At Elysian, I enjoyed excellent relationships with all members of the school community; teaching and support staff worked together closely, and both parents and governors were fully involved in school life. Outside school, my relationship with Frankie was flourishing; we had a civil partnership attended by family and friends, and life was good. As content as I think I had ever been, I decided to retire from teaching and enjoy life!

Two settings, one career

It is interesting to stop and reflect on how you have lived your life. Reflecting on my journey, there are multiple ways in which I have experienced 'two settings'. When I started writing, I thought the difference was between my rural teaching experiences compared to life in the city. Reading it now, it could be interpreted as life in the state-maintained schools versus life in the independent sector. Probably most pertinent is life with Section 28 (my 'don't ask, don't tell' years) compared to life since its repeal (my 'out and proud' phase). For much of my time at Glade, I feared that I would be exposed as a gay teacher, while by the time I left Elysian I was recognised as a school leader who is gay.

My career spanned four schools, two state-maintained and two independent. As a teacher I loved sharing my subject and getting the best out of pupils of all abilities. I also relished extra-curricular activities, contributing to young people's holistic development, and my role as a tutor offering guidance and supporting their wellbeing. As a leader, I consider myself fortunate to have held senior roles in three fantastic schools, enabling me to grow from my early instructional style to a more open, collegial one. Was I a Courageous Leader? That would be for others to say, but I have certainly had a fulfilling career, and one I would not change for the world.

Advice for an LGBT inclusive school from Yvonne Marsden

Schools commonly have a senior leader responsible for staff development, but often this person does not have time to personalise the staff development for each teacher. For me, best practice is for this person to meet every member of staff for 15 to 30 minutes every year to really get to know them. With an open approach, characterised by a professional curiosity and taking a genuine interest in individuals, this can result in all members of staff, including LGBT ones, feeling valued and being given suitable professional development opportunities. This also helps to create a metaphorical safe space; something needed by many teachers on their journeys, be it due to sexuality or gender-based issues, or issues that have the potential to affect every teacher, such as depression or bereavement.

REFERENCES

Benn, M. (2012) *School wars: the battle for Britain's education*. London: Verso.

Clarke, G. (1996) 'Conforming and contesting with (a) difference: how lesbian students and teachers manage their identities', *International Studies in Sociology of Education* 6 (2) pp. 191–209.

Lee, C. (2019a) 'Fifteen years on: the legacy of Section 28 for LGBT+ teachers in English schools', *Sex Education* 19 (6) pp. 675–690.

Lee, C. (2019b) 'How do lesbian, gay and bisexual teachers experience UK rural school communities?', *Social Sciences* 8 (9) pp. 249–258.

Smith, A. M. (1994) *New right discourse on race and sexuality: Britain, 1968–1990*. Cambridge: Cambridge University Press.

3: The perspectives of a New Zealander: the power of community, connections and collaborations between queer teachers

Jerome Cargill

Jerome Cargill began his teaching career in his native New Zealand. In the first of three contributions to this book, Jerome compares his upbringing and early teaching career in New Zealand with his more recent roles as a teacher in London. Throughout his story, he reflects on the importance of good communication and a strong sense of community in helping queer teachers to become their authentic selves in the school workplace.

Tēnā koutou katoa
Ko Matairangi te māunga
Ko Te Awa Kairangi te awa
Nō Whanganui-a-Tara ahau
Kei London tōku kāinga ināianei
Ko Jerome Cargill tōku ingoa
Nō reira, tēnā koutou, tēnā koutou, tēnā koutou katoa

In New Zealand, where I am from, this is the traditional Māori way of introducing yourself. It is called a *pepeha*, and translated it tells you that I am from Wellington, New Zealand, where my mountain and river growing up were Mount Victoria and the Hutt River, and I am now living in London. I am Pākehā (a white New Zealander of European descent), but like many New Zealanders I am passionate about our bicultural society, and participate in traditions such as formally introducing myself with my *pepeha* at appropriate occasions.

People, relationships and the interconnectedness of our different contexts are fundamental to Māori. These values that I have been raised with are an important foundation to this chapter, and therefore felt like an appropriate starting point to share some of my story.

I started teaching in New Zealand when I was 21 years old, unprepared for how to navigate my sexuality in a professional setting. While I told friends I was comfortable coming out as a teacher, the truth was that this was something I held a deep anxiety about.

My approach had been shaped by my school experience as a teen-ager, where homophobia was normal in the traditional all-boys school I attended. I had also been influenced by the wider culture of the early 2000s, which offered few opportunities to discover positive role models. As a trainee teacher, I chose to focus on my practice and not get caught up by this. I chose not to lie but to avoid (something that I now acknowledge is actually another form of lying). On one particular occasion where I was being observed teaching I made a comment, or maybe a gesture, which lead to my university mentor pulling me aside and angrily denouncing how I had flaunted my sexuality in front of the class. I was told I was being deliberately provocative and my personal life was none of the students' business.

All of this meant that I decided to keep my sexuality invisible when I took up my first teaching post. I didn't want my difference to be noticed.

In my first school during my first year of teaching I discovered, quite by accident, that there were other queer staff. The first I found out about by overhearing a conversation in the photocopy room. My ears pricked up when the teachers casually referred to Craig as being gay. This surprised me a lot because at this point, I had only met one Craig in the school and had no idea that there were in fact two. When I finally resolved this later on and met the second Craig, what I had overheard in the photocopy room made far more sense. While I remained silent in this instance, the casual acceptance of Craig by the other staff members made me feel more welcome.

In time, a couple of people from the top of my hypothetical list of potential queer staff members referred to their same-gendered partners around the lunch table. Again I remained silent. Having no partner at this point made it harder to casually enter into this conversation and I was not ready to make any announcement.

Eventually I found out that a colleague I was working closely with in my department was a lesbian. Again this came up in a casual way, but importantly this was someone who I was growing close to and someone who I felt like I could come out to at the right time.

The way I approached this was ridiculous when I reflect on it. My naivety was clear through the way I felt like I had to justify this part of myself and the levels of preparation that went into this moment. It also reflected where I was at in my journey. In one of our weekly meetings I asked for a private word and we went in search of an unoccupied room. Appropriately, we ended up in the drama department's costume cupboard and fashioned two seats out of random props that were lying on the floor. I delivered my speech, which my colleague met with heart-warming acceptance as well as suggesting that she had already pretty much assumed. It was such a relief to finally come out to someone at school.

I then heard about the seven other queer staff members (I had only found three) and learned about their annual 'family' dinners. It wasn't so much a secret society, just one I hadn't picked up on. I came out of that costume closet completely changed and a different teacher. It was also the first time I had ever talked with another queer teacher about coming out to students.

Beyond school I had been out for three years, but I hadn't found a community in all that time; now through my colleagues at school I had found my first queer family. Through them I learned a lot more about the complex feelings that I had been navigating. I found that a lot of what had been repressing my confidence was a form of shame. Society had been teaching me that my queerness was something to hide; a transgression that I should not be proud of. I formed friendships with colleagues who had felt similar things but were confident and proud in a way I looked up to. I met the long-term partners of three of my colleagues; this was the first time I had seen healthy queer relationships, which was so important to me after three years of unsuccessful dating.

I never technically came out to a class for several years. There were certainly students that knew: an end of the year 'thanks for being our princess' card was a giveaway, as were the rumours I was vaguely aware of but too terrified to learn any more about. It took a long time to stop thinking of my sexuality as something that should be hidden; something that I shouldn't flaunt. I remember feeling uncomfortable and nervous when any queer content or issue came up in class, even shaking at times, avoiding saying anything that could possibly expose me and moving the conversation on as quickly as possible.

Coming out is a political act. It defies an assumption that heteronormativity imposes on all of us.

My discovery of the power of this act came when for the first time a student came out to me. I don't know whether he sensed an ally, or whether I was just in the right place at the right time, but it triggered a huge change in me as I came to understand the symbolic importance of being honest about myself in front of the students I was teaching. I had no positive role models when I was 14, but here was an opportunity to help others by being open and proud about myself.

With the support of two other staff from my queer family at school, we set up a support group. Approaching students we knew of and others that the guidance counsellor helped connect us with, we established a safe space in secret weekly gatherings. We were small at first, but the opportunity for the students to discuss the issues they were facing without stigma was invaluable. Many of those students were dealing with complex issues; some didn't feel safe at home while others were struggling with their religion, and all were on the difficult journey of coming to terms with their identity.

These conversations were also helpful to me as I came to understand the importance of being my authentic self with students. In a way, I myself was at the time still discovering my authentic self.

As the group grew, we made plans to advertise its existence. This led to myself and another colleague delivering an assembly. In this assembly

I talked about queer people being everywhere in our society; I said they are 'in the news, on the TV, in your communities, in your families, in your classrooms, and two are speaking to you today.'

My journey to being a role model where I could be my authentic self could not have been achieved without the support and the queer community that I was lucky enough to find at my first school. It took me a long time to close the dissonance between my actions in the classroom and the values that I held. It took the power of community and some important connections with others to get me to where I am today.

Connections and community have been essential for every step of the queer rights movement. Visibility was one of the most powerful triggers for change in the history of the fight for equal rights, which relied on queer people being able to find each other, share their experiences and work together to enact change.

There is a distinct power in being visible as a community. One person standing up for change can be a powerful catalyst, but the power of thousands on the street campaigning against injustice and discrimination is what created the momentum to turn a protest into a movement. Likewise, a single queer teacher speaking out in a school may start conversations, but a community of teachers that take action for the inclusion of gender and sexual minorities is what can create true and meaningful change.

The communities I speak of can consist of a variety of people, including allies, but the argument I want to make here is for the importance of queer communities. My personal experience would not have been the same if I had only encountered straight allies and didn't learn from the experiences of other queer people. It is really vital that we encourage and support single queer voices, and help connect them to meaningful communities.

Our modern world makes it so much easier to connect with established communities. The role of the internet and social media in creating connections is vital. A queer student who started mid-year approached me in her first few days at school after googling the school and finding a blog post I had written about supporting queer students. She then joined the support group and thrived through the connections she made, enabled by the online information that she'd found. After I was fortunate enough to appear on a news programme about being an out role model at my school, a number of teachers across New Zealand reached out to me through online networks to connect and share their stories.

To find connections, teachers and students need visibility, which is why high-profile events like pride parades, queer conferences, LGBTI+ union networks and other opportunities to connect are so vital. Part of the purpose of these events is to make visible the different communities and connections that are available. Connecting through shared experience helps to validate our difference and create strength in the face of othering and discrimination.

The queer community could be thought of as an imagined community. Benedict Anderson (1991) developed the idea of an imagined community to explain how nationalism can be thought of as something that is socially constructed. The concept helps us to understand the idea of nationhood and a deep relationship to one's own country. Coming out as a queer person is like joining an imagined community. The stereotype of taking in new queens and jokes like earning your 'gay card' perpetuate the idea of a sense of belonging.

But not every aspect of the LGBTI+ community is positive. It can be exclusionary and divisive, as debates around who gets to 'belong' continue with tenacity. Bisexual erasure is one such example, where someone identifying as bisexual might not be accepted in a queer space because they might be in a heterosexual relationship, or because some completely erase the idea of bisexuality as an identity. The disturbing anti-trans rhetoric from both outside and inside the queer community is another example.

Just as the Anderson's 'imagined community' needs continuous interrogation to ensure the concept of nationalism is responsive to today's needs and values, the idea of a queer community needs to also be continuously interrogated. What does the queer community represent? What needs and values does it stand for? These questions need wide and sustained input, but my argument here is for the importance of community and the need to encourage making connections.

In my ten years of teaching, I've had several opportunities to be in spaces exclusively occupied by queer teachers. There is something uniquely meaningful about these experiences; they have been so important to the growth of my queer identity and the journey to rid myself of the shame that helped me hide my identity from others at the start of my career. The following are the three opportunities that meant the most to my personal development.

The first exclusively queer teacher space was the annual 'family' dinners of the seven queer teachers at my first school. As a young person, this was a new experience for me; both as a dinner-party experience and because I was in a room with older queer people. Connecting with older queer people was new to me partly because I hadn't attempted to find this community before, but also because opportunities to connect with this community were hard to access. It was so important to me to see role models living a lifestyle that I aspired to, challenging my heteronormative visions of what it meant to be middle aged and queer. We talked as friends do, sharing stories from the past and plans for the future, and I found myself feeling a comfort that was new to me.

These dinner parties were advertised in whole-staff emails; the aim was to invite any other queer staff in the school that were not visibly out, but also to advertise the presence of queer voices in the school. This was one way of creating visibility.

The second time I found an exclusively queer teacher space was when I joined eight other teachers making up the Post Primary Teachers' Association Rainbow Taskforce in New Zealand. The group advocated for and supported change to make schools safer for queer teachers and students. One of the key ways of doing this was delivering 'Safer schools for all' workshops in schools around the country, which addressed things like how to challenge homophobia and how to make the curriculum more inclusive.

The group developed my understanding of the political discourse around my identity. It helped me to see that I was relatively privileged to have not encountered much homophobia in the workplace, as my eyes were opened to the challenges that many other teachers face. It was again the sense of shared experience and connection that this group created which helped me with my own personal growth, as I learned more about my identity in relation to others.

The third time I found an exclusively queer teacher space was in London when I signed up for the Courageous Leaders course. Once again I walked into a room full of queer educators and I felt a unique power. The room was half filled with participants who were at an early stage in their careers, and the other half with mentors who were more experienced, many in senior leadership positions. This opportunity to collaborate, share experiences and connect with queer teachers was meaningful on many levels. For the participants, it offered access to a new queer community with a range of experiences. For the mentors, it offered opportunities to continue their positive work in providing support for other teachers as they attempted to grow in their own careers.

Within the Courageous Leaders programme there is an explicit effort to address the barriers that queer teachers are facing. Case studies from past participants on the course speak of the 'sense of LGBT community that was nurtured quickly in the group' and how it was 'inspiring to hear their stories and how they were making an impact in their own schools'. Just as the most important lessons might involve the learning experienced *outside* the curriculum, it is the conversations that happen outside the content of the course that are often some of the most valuable. This is a unique opportunity for queer teachers in a heteronormative education system.

The key characteristics of these three teacher spaces, in addition to their uniquely queer identities, are the supportive, collaborative environments they fostered and the diverse ages and experiences they brought together. The structures of all three experiences cultivated supportive behaviour in informal and formal ways. Explicit mentoring is one way of shaping an environment that focuses on growth, but the practised values of support and inclusion is what made these spaces special to me.

But perhaps the most important characteristic is that all three required an invitation, and an opportunity to be part of them. I wouldn't have been part of these experiences if people had not reached out to me or if I had not found an advert for them.

All of these queer teacher groups I have been part of have been eclectic, bringing together people with different experiences and of different ages. In the Courageous Leaders course in particular, it was powerful to have multiple generations of teachers together in the same space to share stories. Some teachers had been directly impacted by Section 28, which prevented teachers from talking about homosexuality at school in any way that promoted the lifestyle as acceptable. It felt so relevant to connect to those experiences and understand our history; particularly how the ripples are still impacting us today.

This mixture of generations is one difference that was notable about the Courageous Leaders group, but further to that there were teachers with experience of rural and urban schools, faith-based and secular schools, and teaching within the UK and beyond. These diverse experiences coming together in a supportive environment creates the sense of community, which is empowering for all.

The more understanding we have of others – their challenges, their experiences, and their feelings – the better off we are.

From these experiences I have shared and their underpinning ideas, some core beliefs have emerged. The primary underlining idea is that schools need to take responsibility for providing safe, supportive spaces for queer teachers.

While I have emphasised the importance of queer spaces and queer connections, it is not solely the responsibility of queer teachers to make other queer teachers feel comfortable: it is everyone's responsibility. Any medium-sized school is statistically likely to have several queer teachers, although this might not always be the case. But even if there are no out teachers at your school, asking the question, 'Is our school creating a safe and supportive environment for all teachers to express their sexual or gender identity?' is fundamental to creating an inclusive environment.

Creating positive visibility is the first step. As a supply teacher, I walked into many schools without any knowledge of their culture; however, the difference it made to sit in reception at the beginning of the day and see a pride flag or a Stonewall poster was immense. Unfortunately these instances were rare.

Of course, inclusion is more than just a poster on the wall (although this is a valuable start). Inclusion is visible in so many ways, from the language people address you with to the way people position their bodies when they interact with you. Inclusion is evident in every element in any school.

The challenge for all schools and professionals working within them is to ask themselves: what is the experience of others in this space? Is it a safe, inclusive space for all? And how do they know?

Most schools have a list of values that are incorporated into their vision, some of which suggest that the school should be safe and inclusive for all. But how are these values experienced by a person walking into the school for the first time? How does a visitor to the school know that they are walking into an inclusive school?

Schools should then consider how they are structured so that queer people may connect with each other. How might people new to the school find that community? Is there a formal group, and if so, how is this advertised? Is there a key person that is leading on this, and if so how does one find that person?

The benefits of creating strong inclusive environments can be felt well beyond the LGBTI+ community. To promote inclusion of LGBTI+ people is to promote the values of inclusion that can benefit all. LGBTI+ people need to be included and celebrated in every school, and one way of achieving this is to promote meaningful communities and connections.

Advice for an LGBTI+ inclusive school from Jerome Cargill

Evaluate your school's spaces for positive visibility. How does a queer person new to these spaces know they are safe, included and welcome?

4: Don't always judge a book by its cover
Hannah Wickens

In this chapter, Hannah Wickens reflects on the initial anxieties she had as a lesbian teacher working with Muslim colleagues she wrongly assumed would reject her same-sex relationship. Hannah also explores how since coming out, she has been empowered to set up an LGBT anti-bullying group for pupils at her school.

When I began my career in education, I was working as a teaching assistant for a supply agency in East London. As the work was fairly flexible and I didn't have a permanent base, I didn't really disclose any information about my personal life to the people I worked with. At the time I had been out for about four years and was in a long-term relationship, but I wasn't really part of my school's community to an extent where I felt comfortable enough to be out at work. Even when I secured a permanent position in a Year 3 class, I worked closely with a cis male Muslim teacher and just never felt brave enough to come out at work. We had a fantastic professional relationship but it remained exactly that. I also never lied to him because he never asked or assumed anything about my personal life – he just never asked and I didn't tell.

I moved schools and completed my teacher training. The atmosphere in my new school was different: more diverse and more open-minded. Almost instantly I knew I was in a safe space. Completing my teacher training and having my own class for the first time gave me a sense of accomplishment, and I was more comfortable in my own skin. I felt however that I couldn't be open and honest about my identity with the cis female Muslim teaching assistants who I worked with daily, who are an asset to our local and school community. I assumed that they wouldn't want to hear about my personal life, or they'd think differently about me if they knew I was gay because of their religion. I regret that now because they do know through word of mouth, and have accepted me for who I am, even bringing home-made cooking in for me and my girlfriend. It was my own insecurities that held me back from being open and honest to begin with. Since then, being in a culture of visibility and openness among staff has been a very freeing experience and one that is contrary to my initial experiences as a teaching assistant.

Throughout the last two years I have been leading personal, social and health education in my school; something I have a growing passion for. I think the new relationships, health and sex education (RSE) framework that will be introduced from September 2020 is a huge step in the right direction for schools. From September 2020, all primary schools in England will be required to teach relationships education, all secondary schools in England will be required to teach relationships and sex education, and all schools in England will be required to teach health education that is inclusive of LGBT relationships. At primary level, the guidance states that all primary schools should teach about different families, which 'can include for example, single parent families, LGBT parents, families headed by grandparents', etc. At secondary level, the guidance states that 'sexual orientation and gender identity should be explored at a timely point' and that 'there should be an equal opportunity to explore the features of stable and healthy same-sex relationships', which 'should be integrated appropriately into the RSE programme, rather than addressed separately or in only one lesson' (Department for Education, 2019, p. 20).

Although I am not in a senior leadership position, I am fortunate to be able to make whole-school changes. I have set up Rainbow Ambassadors at my school, which is a student-led anti-bullying group. I have also rewritten our curriculum so that children are exposed to diversity and different types of families throughout their time in primary. Normalising diversity is something that can support our young people to become more open-minded and supportive of each other no matter what. Embedding this in primary can only support their emotional development into secondary.

With parental engagement and hostilities in Newham being influenced by events in Birmingham, it is a challenging time to champion this work, but I feel ready to take what comes. I find it worrying that teachers and senior leaders are being put in a position where we have to defend equality and defend fundamental British rights. Inclusive RSE will help all children and young people to grow up with respectful attitudes towards people who are different to them, and help to tackle the prejudice-based bullying that remains all too common in some of our schools. Inclusive RSE will also support children and young people to know when to ask for help, and will overall help to create a safe and supportive environment for all children, young people and adults.

It's a long road but we're on the right track. Being out to students is the next step in my journey towards total transparency and being a positive role model in my school. We cannot cherry pick which equality we believe in. Equality means everyone has equal value, equal rights and equal opportunities, and no person is superior based on this criteria. Children have no confusion as to what equality means when it is explained to them simply, and they deserve to know about all the different types of people that exist in our society. It's heart-breaking that adult fears and ignorance are influencing the minds of the young people we are trying our very best to support and nurture.

Advice for an LGBT inclusive school from Hannah Wickens

Actively promote a safe and inclusive environment through policy and action. Celebrate diversity and do not tolerate discrimination of any kind. Support staff members that encounter any form of prejudice from parents or staff, making no exceptions. Provide current and relevant training to all staff, to encourage confidence in understanding policy and using current vocabulary that supports LGBT students and staff.

REFERENCES

Department for Education (2019) *Relationships education, relationships and sex education (RSE) and health education: draft statutory guidance for governing bodies, proprietors, head teachers, principals, senior leadership teams, teachers.* London: The Stationary Office.

5: The double whammy
Niamh McNabb

In this powerful and moving story, Niamh explores her gender and sexuality histories (her double whammy). She reflects on the challenges she faced in becoming her authentic self and, crucially, the way in which her school supported her at times of considerable challenge.

Let's start at the end. At the time of writing (late 2019), I've spent over 20 years working in education and now manage guidance staff in a large sixth-form college in Cambridge, where I'm also the equality and diversity lead, in the safeguarding team, and involved in the college pride club. I've just spent almost four years as a trustee with The Kite Trust, an amazing charity that works with young LGBT+ people. I'm out and proud and I'm trying to be the role model I wish I had. But it hasn't always been that way. In my first year on the Courageous Leaders team, I was asked to talk to a group of middle-leaders in education about my life, the barriers I faced and how I overcame them. I called the talk 'Why I'm not on benefits, in prison or dead'. This is part of that story.

Like many LGBT+ people, I knew I was different from a very young age. I was assigned male at birth and this was never a comfortable fit. My femininity was somewhat obvious and my extended family assumed I was gay from childhood. I always found this difficult to understand until I was much older and I met a transwoman who had not transitioned, who I too assumed was a 'gay man'. As I grew up, I knew I was attracted to both boys and girls and this blurred with my gender identity, causing a lot of confusion at times. My attraction to others was complex and I often over-analysed it in the context of my gender rather than just going with it. Gender and sexuality are distinct and different but inextricably connected, and when neither conforms to social norms it can be very difficult, especially when there are no role models. Later in life I came across this being called 'the double whammy'.

Context is important here. I grew up in the 70s and 80s on a council estate in a small town in Northern Ireland. My family situation was very unusual in that my parents were not of the same religion. I was brought up as a Catholic in a Protestant estate in a Protestant town; I went to a Catholic primary school and a Protestant secondary school. I lost my religion in my early teens and my faith not long after that, and I'm now a confirmed atheist. My maternal grandfather was an Orangeman and a relative on my father's side was a senior figure in the IRA in the 60s and 70s (and probably beyond but details were scarce, even from him).

The Troubles caused significant financial problems in the province and when Margaret Thatcher became prime minister in 1979, things got worse. The American owners of the cotton spinning factory in which my father worked pulled out, and in 1981 he lost his job. He never worked again. Alcohol became his primary raison d'etre. We relied on benefits throughout the 80s, as did many families on the estate, supplemented by my mother's earnings from washing dishes. My formative years were spent living in a society in which I didn't fit, as I have done ever since. My mother was, and is, remarkable. She held everything together. I never felt that we had a hard life. Others on the estate had it better than us but there were very many who had it so much worse. Nowadays at least two thirds of the kids, including me, would have had contact with safeguarding staff at school.

I always wanted to be a doctor, probably due to the frequent contact I had with the medical profession due to my poor health, which was always problematic. I was fortunate to do well in my eleven-plus and went to the local grammar school. University was my aim, my escape, my way out. Like most LGBT+ people my mental health was not at its best. Many think that this is because we are queer but it's not. It is because of society's lack of acceptance of those who are different. My plans for medicine got scuppered in sixth form and somehow I ended up starting a physics degree at the University of Nottingham in 1990. The first time I ever left Ireland was for my interview and the second was for the start of term. My mother saved up so that I could fly and it was the first time I'd ever been on a plane.

My mental health continued to deteriorate. I accessed counselling but I just couldn't tell anyone about my burden. My risk-taking behaviour increased. During one particularly difficult evening in 1991, I called the Samaritans and told them I was transsexual. The terms 'trans' and 'transgender' were not in use then. I freaked out and spiralled into a breakdown that I was lucky to get through. I didn't tell anyone for another 11 years and instead I came out as gay, because at least I was telling people I was different. Being gay was more acceptable, but I realised fairly quickly that this didn't fit and then came out as bisexual. This was more accurate, if not the whole picture, and has been the way I've described my sexuality for most of the time since then. Sadly bisexuality has never been accepted by society in quite the same way that homosexuality has and many misunderstandings still exist.

Upon graduating from university, I went back to Northern Ireland to recover and regroup. Photography had been a passion from the age of 17. I worked in a camera shop for a few years when at school and it was an area in which I now wanted to work. I got a job with a photographer as a studio assistant. After nine months I had passed my driving test and saved a little money. I bought a one-way flight to London, packed a rucksack, and left with £200 cash in my pocket and the phone number of a school friend who had a flat. It was only the second time I had ever been to London. I have lived in England ever since.

I started looking for work and within a month or so I got a job as a photographer at Madame Tussauds taking commercial portraits. It was hard work in a busy and strict environment and I hated it, but I made some good friends and it was also an exciting time. I had a long-term girlfriend, who I had been together with on and off since I was 15. After chicken pox and then a back injury I accidentally ended up living with her. That wasn't our plan.

When I was 25, I got a job as a photographic adviser at Nikon's UK headquarters in Kingston upon Thames, where I worked for three and a half years. I was a rebel (it's in my blood) and I do remember my boss telling me that I didn't realise how lucky I was to work there. It took me many years to find out he was right.

My mental health continued to be poor and this caused problems. I had private medical insurance with my job, which paid for therapy. I was eventually diagnosed with clinical depression, having suffered for over ten years. I discussed my gender issues but I was never completely open. The therapist took a Freudian approach and tried to tell me it was due to my poor relationship with my father and positive relationship with my mother, no matter how many times I told him I felt this way before any awareness of the issues surrounding my father.

My partner (I never called her my girlfriend) knew part of the picture by this time, and I was starting to explore my gender. Nowadays I would be described as gender non-conforming or maybe gender fluid. My partner was called Alex and when colleagues met her for the first time they were shocked because they expected a man. We were part of a group of twenty-somethings enjoying London but my risk-taking continued, in its many and varied forms, and my mental health deteriorated further. If it wasn't for an intervention, I wouldn't be here today.

I looked for new work challenges and got myself a job as a staff writer on *Practical Photography* magazine in Peterborough, which I did for about two years. I was 27 and I was one of the country's foremost photographic experts. I was travelling the country, and at times Europe, and I had two publishers wanting books. My partner and I split because I had to somehow deal with my identity. I soon ended up in a relationship with a bi woman. It was like no relationship I'd ever had, transcending gender and sexuality. She remained my partner until after my transition and was instrumental in helping me throughout.

I found publishing to be a highly competitive and high-pressured environment and decided it wasn't for me. I worked in aerial photography for a while and continued to write as a freelancer, but it didn't work out. I am not cut out to be self-employed. In 1999, having again relied on benefits for a few months, I applied for a part-time job teaching photography at the local general further education college. In September 1999 I started teaching two lessons per week, and in January 2000 I started running the department. My poor health and resulting absences were problematic. I had missed lots of days at school, university and other jobs, but now the impact on others was much greater. I had another major depressive episode. It was clear that the episodes were getting longer and closer together, and in my first year of teaching there was another life-saving intervention. In 2002 I realised I just couldn't go on anymore. I had no strength left, no reserves, no resilience. I was beaten and I had to transition or I had to die. That was the choice.

I did not want to be trans. Throughout my life I had seen the negative press about trans people. I remembered the stories about the model Caroline Cossey well. I heard the jokes and saw the hatred, even from people I called friends. I didn't want to be one of those people; I just wanted to get on with my life. I had no issues with my sexuality – in fact I was out and proud even when being bi wasn't cool – but the same could not be said for my gender identity. Looking back now, even as a very young child I knew I should have been a girl. And I don't mean wearing pink and playing with dolls (I actually like 'boy's' toys and am not a fan of pink). It was physical dysphoria and a social disconnection, but I had no real frame of reference to help understand it, or the language to explain it.

My transition was planned with military precision. It became my everything and dominated almost every part of my life. My college was great, mostly due to my boss. She ensured I had control over the process. She acted as an intermediary between me and HR at times and protected me from some colleagues' ignorant questions and comments. She helped me plan and risk-assess, and supported me when things were difficult. She was always there for me. We quickly became very close and she is now my dearest friend. In advance of my social transition, I informed staff through the bulletin and my tutees in tutorial. I will never forget that day. I was sick with anxiety but my students were so amazing.

I left before the Easter holidays as male and returned as female. Every day was stressful. The students continued to impress me as did most of my colleagues, although a few were quite malicious at times. My GP too was amazing. There was little access to support on the NHS so I borrowed the money and went private. My GP ensured I could get my hormones on the NHS and she arranged access to an incredible counsellor who had previously helped me in my pursuit of self-preservation. The Gender Recognition Act was two years away and the Equality Act eight years, yet I could change the gender on my driving licence and passport. I self-identified. I used women's changing rooms and toilets and never have I had an issue.

After a couple of years I decided I needed a new challenge at work and a career plan. I changed subject, moving into science and maths, and this involved moving to the main site of the large college in which I worked. That's when my problems really started. I was getting harassed and being called names in the corridors by students. It was awful. It made me ill. I became anxious every day and started to avoid certain parts of the college. The senior staff in college did not handle it well and after two years I left to start at my current sixth form.

Before my transition I was very confident, but afterwards I lost it all. I became very nervous and anxious about new situations or people I didn't know. I was lucky in that I had very few bad experiences with strangers, but I was still cautious. I had lots of friends and I lost most of them too. I told my university friends before the event and they never contacted me again. Interestingly my LGB friends left my life the quickest. My boss at the time of transitioning is the only friend I have from the time before. My family found it hard. My mother was fine about my sexuality but this was different. She thought it was dangerous, she'd watched too much *Jeremy Kyle*, but in truth medical transitions can be risky. In time she came around and quickly we were closer than ever.

In 2005 I jumped through the hoops and paid my money to get a Gender Recognition Certificate, which in turn got me a new birth certificate, so I was fully protected by the Gender Recognition Act. Interestingly I have never used either of those documents since, but at least I knew I had full legal protection.

When I transitioned, 'living in stealth' was the aim of most trans people: being able to live in society without anyone knowing. It isn't about being secretive, but being private. It's about just getting on with life. When I started at my new college that is what I decided to do. I told the HR manager and the principal and that's it. I had made it. I had done it. I was living as a cis woman. I had transitioned and moved on. There were actually times I forgot I was trans and it was magical, but then something would happen that would remind me. I found I became quiet during conversations about sharing pasts. I couldn't lie so I said nothing. I lived like this for six years, but over time I became more isolated. I didn't develop close friendships and I was alone even in company.

By now I was a senior member of the pastoral team and increasing numbers of students were coming out as trans. It was becoming a talking point among staff and people were asking for my advice. I found myself trying not to be too knowledgeable. Oh, the irony. It didn't take long before I just couldn't do it anymore and I talked to SLT about coming out. Some supported me in making the decision and some said I shouldn't (they were trying to protect me). I knew I had to come out but quite frankly I was scared. Once I told people there would be no going back and I'd been burned before. The college paid for me to have counselling to help me with the decision and the process of coming out. This wasn't anywhere nearly as difficult as the first time I came out as trans, but it still made me anxious. I decided I wanted to be an LGBT+ role model again, as I had in my previous college. I wanted to be the role model I never had. I therefore came out and became involved in the college's pride club, and then became a trustee of The Kite Trust. My boss told me about a project I might be interested in and I enrolled on Courageous Leaders programme. I was a professional queer and life was good. I even started the complicated process of dating again.

Society's views of trans people seemed to be becoming more positive, but then the consultation around the Gender Recognition Act started in 2004 and it all changed. There was misinformation and misunderstanding, especially around self-identification. Trans hate groups sprang up. Trans women were being portrayed as predators and trans men as lesbians who had been brainwashed by the patriarchy. Somehow we were trying to corrupt children and reduce women's rights. No matter that there is not a finite amount of rights – increasing the rights of trans people does not reduce the rights of others.

Let's be very clear: there is no single trans voice. Trans people hold a variety of views, just like everyone else. The rhetoric that used to surround the 'gay agenda' in the 1980s about predatory behaviour and hypersexuality is being repeated in 2020, this time with the trans community as its focus. No one can make someone else trans. Trans people take an interest in the support of young trans people because we were young trans people. We share their pain.

I am now a role model to young LGBT+ people. I understand them in ways that other staff can't. There has been a blurring of my job and my identity and this has enabled me to provide a unique level of support to students, families and staff. However, that empathy can come at a cost: when one of our trans students recently took their own life it almost destroyed me. I know that pain so, so well. Again, my college provided me with appropriate support and I work with SLT to reflect on my role. I am never left to deal with anything by myself.

I'm now part of the team that runs Courageous Leaders and I love it. I have gained confidence and met some remarkable and inspirational people. Through my involvement in the programme and my work with LGBT+ students, I was given the role of equality and diversity lead at my college. I am now an authentic leader. I have always been reflective. I have learned from the social deprivation, religious sectarianism, homophobia, biphobia, transphobia, misogyny, risk-taking behaviour, domestic violence and familial alcoholism. Every time I was knocked down, and there were a fair few times, I learned from it and I came back stronger. My barriers have become strengths. Just to be clear, I do not feel sorry for myself. My past has played no part in forming my queer identity, but it has been instrumental in forming my personality, in particular my rather dark sense of humour.

I'm in an unusual situation in that I have had gay and straight relationships with both men and women. I am a bisexual woman with a trans history. I have never used the word transgender to describe myself, or the word transsexual since that phone call in 1991. I don't like either of those words. I'm in relationship with a fabulous woman, a cis lesbian, who just sees me like any other woman. I continue to use the word bisexual (I'm fine with pansexual too) because I don't want anyone to think I have ever been straight, but ultimately I describe myself as queer because it's shorter. I like the word queer and I reclaim it for all of us whose sexuality and/or gender identity do not fit with the social norms. I am queer and I have nothing to prove and nothing to hide.

Advice for an LGBT+ inclusive school from Niamh McNabb

Give LGBT+ staff ownership of their situation. Consult LGBT+ staff about decisions that may affect them. Do not just act in what you think might be their best interests because the opposite might be true. Protect LGBT+ staff from discrimination, but don't keep problems secret from them – it's usually better if they know the truth. And remember: not all LGBT+ people are the same or have the same views on LGBT+ issues.

6: Parent power and the rural school community
Catherine Lee

In this chapter, Catherine Lee describes an incident that led her to leave teaching for good after more than 20 years in the profession. She explores the incompatibility of her private and professional identities, and reflects on the impact of homophobic and heteronormative discursive practices in the workplace and school community, and on her health, wellbeing and identity.

In this chapter, I explore how I prospered as an assistant headteacher at a village school for almost ten years by censoring my sexuality and carefully managing the intersection between my private and professional identities. However, when a malicious and homophobic neighbour with children at the school (let's call him Mr Freeman) exposed my sexuality to the headteacher, I learned the extent to which the rural school community privileged and protected the heteronormative discourse.

In July 2009, my then civil partner and I first encountered our new neighbour, Mr Freeman. He was a father of five, and had recently enrolled three of his children at the local school at which I was assistant headteacher. During that first encounter, Mr Freeman was openly homophobic and threatened us on the doorstep of our cottage. In the months that followed he subjected us to harassment outside our home. He also made an appointment with my headteacher, to 'out' me as a lesbian and allege that I had been staring lustfully at his daughters, aged nine. As a consequence of his behaviour, we sold our home and moved into rented accommodation. I also left teaching. What follows is my account of how exactly this happened.

I lived with my partner, Jo, in rural South East England. We had a house surrounded on three sides by fields belonging to the local Wildlife Trust. We felt lucky to have found a home in such a wonderful location and enjoyed the peace and privacy it afforded us. In June 2009, the neighbouring farmhouse and only other property for half a mile was sold to the Freemans, a family of seven. They moved in and enrolled three of their children at the school at which I was assistant headteacher. The other two children were enrolled at the local primary school, set to follow their siblings to secondary school in due course. The Freemans had a garden of six acres, but placed a trampoline so it immediately abutted our boundary, no more than fifteen feet from our kitchen and living room windows. The Freeman children loved the trampoline, not least, I suspect, because jumping on it gave them an intermittent view of their new teacher, her house, and her female partner.

My partner and I were upset at this intrusion to our privacy. In early July we decided to go and introduce ourselves and welcome the Freemans to the village, hoping in the process for an opportunity to mention the trampoline problem. As we arrived in the driveway, Mrs Freeman was departing in the car. She shouted that she would leave us with her husband George, and would perhaps see us later.

George Freeman showed us around the grounds of his new property, clearly proud of his new acquisition. As we stood in the sunshine with Mr Freeman, coerced into admiring his estate, I struggled to find anything I liked about him. Perhaps this showed. I sensed he felt exactly the same about me.

The conversation remained friendly but Mr Freeman slowly began to step forward into my personal space, holding my gaze throughout. Instinctively, I retreated. Meanwhile my partner sensitively broached the subject of the trampoline, explaining that I was a teacher at the school his children attended and that it was important for his children and for me that professional and personal boundaries did not become blurred. With a flash of aggression, Mr Freeman marched over to the trampoline and dragged it back from our boundary by approximately three feet. Startled by his anger, we thanked him for appreciating our position and did the best we could to round off this encounter in a cordial and neighbourly manner. Our lack of further challenge seemed immediately to calm him and we parted on good terms, with an invitation to their forthcoming housewarming party.

As we walked home, my partner and I talked in anxious whispers, concerned by Mr Freeman's cynical and aggressive response to our request. Once safely back inside we found ourselves continuing our whispered conversation at the top of the stairs, the only place in our house without windows or external doors. Suddenly, vigorous banging on the front door interrupted our conversation. We dashed downstairs to find Mr Freeman, pacing on and off the doorstep. He had changed out of the shorts and T-shirt we had encountered him in minutes before, into full western wear: a Stetson, a checked shirt and cowboy boots. He began to shout that he would not be told what to do by a pair of lesbians and was going to make our lives a 'living misery'. We stood paralysed as he spat out more and more frustrated threats. He said that he had already reported me to my headmaster, though for what he did not say. As he swaggered back down our driveway, we stood on our doorstep in open-mouthed silence, shaken and scared as we watched him stride back to the farm.

I urged Jo to stay inside and to keep our cat, Lily, inside too. I jumped in the car and raced the mile and a half to school, hoping to catch my headteacher before he left for the day. I found him in the corridor about to depart. Relieved and on the verge of tears, I asked if Mr Freeman had phoned the school and carefully recounted some of the earlier incident, without mentioning my sexuality. My headteacher reassured me that he had not phoned, adding that if Mr Freeman was to make a complaint about me, he would tell him 'where to get off'.

The following weeks were unhappy and uncomfortable. Though no further words were exchanged with the Freemans, Mr Freeman pursued and provoked us at every opportunity. He called us 'dykes', 'lezzers' and other homophobic names. He urinated in our garden, appeared at our windows, and tried to run us off the narrow country lanes in his enormous four-wheel drive. We staunchly attempted to enjoy the summer sunshine but we had become an obsession to Mr Freeman. He could not settle if we were outside, and shouted or howled or laughed loudly and inexplicably at us. He threw things over the fence to startle us; on one occasion it was a bucket and on another a bag of clothes pegs.

I was relieved not to be teaching any of them and made a conscious decision to try to remain unaware of them in this setting. I hoped that this would help me to avoid any awkward encounters with them and ensure I was fair and consistent in any chance dealings I did have with them. This was not too difficult to achieve in a school of more than 700 pupils, especially as I was not too sure what they looked like, such was my determination to avoid them at home.

Mr Freeman's aggressive taunts and the trampolining Freeman children made me feel vulnerable and anxious both at home and at school. The more Mr Freeman provoked us, particularly with homophobic names, and the more the children peered into my home and garden, the more convinced I became of the incompatibility of my lesbian and teacher identities. Once the summer holidays began, I started to make plans to escape Mr Freeman and to escape teaching. I began looking for new roles outside teaching, determined that I would never again place myself in such a vulnerable position professionally. I was appointed as an education adviser for the local authority, planning to leave the school that December and commence my new role in January the following year. We also put the house on the market during the summer holidays. Even though I knew that after I left the school, Mr Freeman's ability to inflict damage on me professionally would all but dissipate, neither Jo nor I could tolerate his unpredictable and aggressive behaviour. Although we loved our cottage, our ability to enjoy it had disintegrated. Put simply, regardless of whether I was a teacher at the local school, we felt unsafe in our home and had an urgent need to get as far away from Mr Freeman as possible.

The stress of being subject to harassment by Mr Freeman began to take its toll on me physically and towards the end of the summer holidays, I was admitted to hospital with abdominal pain. Surgery followed for the removal of ovarian cysts that had lain dormant for some time. Recovering from the operation on the hospital ward, I read the local newspaper, and saw for the first time our beloved cottage for sale in the newspaper's property section. The text in our property listing was inaccurate, the directions to the cottage were wrong and the photographs were not those we had approved. I rang the estate agent from my hospital bed and raged at her for the mistakes. As I saw evidence of our home slipping away from us, I felt angry, hopeless and overwhelmed by the loss.

Recovering at home, I did not mourn the end of the summer as I usually did; instead, I counted the weeks until the clocks went back, marking the end of British summer time, hoping to see and hear less of Mr Freeman. I recovered from my operation and in October as the darker evenings descended, I returned to school. Thankfully, Mr Freeman appeared to retreat indoors for the winter and the Freeman family cat became the sole unsettling and symbolic reminder of the hostilities, as he crashed through our cat flap each evening to mark his territory and bully our aged and timid Lily.

As Mr Freeman appeared less interested in us, I wondered whether I had been a little hasty to leave my teaching job and put our house on the market. I was soon to realise I had made entirely the right decision. Shortly after returning to school,my headteacher asked to see me in his office. As we walked together to his room he reassured me that it was nothing to worry about. As I closed the door, my head said simply, 'he's been in'. I immediately knew exactly who 'he' was and barraged my head with questions. Mr Freeman had come into school to tell my head that I was a lesbian and to express his concern that I was teaching. He had qualified his concern by alleging that I had been staring lustfully at his 9-year-old daughters. My head said that Mr Freeman 'had a real problem' with me and recommended that I 'get out of the house as soon as possible'. I laughed with nerves. I had never mentioned to my head that I was a lesbian. 'What did you say to him?' I asked. I wanted to trust that my head had followed through on his earlier promise of telling Mr Freeman 'where to get off'. Instead I listened as he recounted that he had told Mr Freeman that I would be leaving the school in a few weeks' time.

I remained in my head's office unsure of how to proceed. He had always been good to me and I really liked him. I remained in the room, trying to form sentences, trying to think of words that would stress my disapproval without destroying our positive relationship. Now impatient and obviously wishing that I and this situation would go away, my head said that I was overreacting and that it was 'no big deal'. When I finally managed to speak, it was a lame attempt to assert myself. I told my head that I hoped that if I ever reported Mr Freeman to the police, he would support me by telling the police about this visit. Annoyed at my challenge, he snapped that his priority was to get along with Mr Freeman, particularly as he had so many children passing through the school.

I reflected on the conversation as I left the head's office to return to my own. Mr Freeman's allegation that I had been staring lustfully at his daughters did not seem outrageous to my head. He had felt unable or unprepared to challenge it. I started to worry that other colleagues and other parents would deem the accusation feasible.

After a sleepless night, I decided that I ought to record the events somewhere in case Mr Freeman escalated his activities at school or at home. In school the next morning I confided in the school counsellor, who told me of the existence of a County Council Incident form. I got a copy from the school secretary and read through the pro-forma.

The form was generic and designed primarily for the reporting of work-related injuries such as slipping on a wet floor or receiving a back injury from excessive lifting. There was a single tick box to denote that an emotional injury had been sustained and three lines in which to describe the nature of the injury. I drafted my account of events several times, struggling to include all the key points succinctly. Eventually I entered the following wording on the form:

> Since July 2009 I have been subject to harassment from a neighbour. On 1/12/09 the neighbour came to the school to inform the headteacher that I was a lesbian and had been staring at his daughters who are pupils here. Mr [headteacher's name] warned me that this parent was homophobic and recommended that I get out of the house I'm selling as soon as possible.

I returned the form to the secretary, who explained that my head had to countersign the form before it could be submitted. I left it with her and returned to my office. Moments later I received an email which read:

> We need to talk further about this Catherine because I am unhappy
> to sign the form as it stands. I feel you have misquoted me.
> Regards
> [Headteacher's name]

I set off to find the head and met him walking along the corridor on his way to find me. He returned my form to me littered with red-pen annotations, and reiterated that he was not prepared to sign it off. He presented me with two choices: accept his wording on the annotated form, or submit my original form with an accompanying letter from him which would state that I had misquoted him. I asked how I had misquoted him, and after an exasperated sigh was told that he had been speaking to me about the visit of Mr Freeman informally, repeating that he had to get along with him after I had left the school. He added that my problem with Mr Freeman was not really a school issue. Frustrated and resentful, I reluctantly agreed that I would reword the form as per his annotations.

My head escorted me to the secretary to collect a second incident form and told me that the original must be returned. I complied, aware I had already taken a photocopy. I returned to my office and rewrote the whole form, complete with the wording my head insisted on:

> On 1/12/09 a neighbour came into school and mentioned my
> living arrangements to my headteacher. I feel very upset about this.

I stared at the completed form. The wording made the incident sound paltry and inconsequential. The homophobia no longer existed; the harassment no longer existed; the allegation of staring no longer existed; the warning to get out of my home no longer existed. I screwed up the form and threw it across my office.

After keeping the incident a secret for several days, I mentioned it to a colleague who knew I was gay and whom I trusted. She was sympathetic and I found that I gained strength and confidence from her support. Consequently I also told another colleague I was out to, taking comfort from her supportive responses. Recounting my ordeal to the blunt and pragmatic head of mathematics, she suggested to me that the head ought to have suspended me pending an enquiry. She added that any allegation of this nature should be investigated. She intended to reassure me that, as I had not been called to account for the allegation, it was not a serious issue. I did not feel reassured. I believed at the time that she saw me as a paedophile.

Inevitably, the Freeman children began to tell their friends about my 'living arrangements'. A teaching assistant told me that I had been the topic of conversation in the class she was attached to. Before long the walk from my classroom to my office, the staffroom or the playground was tortuous. Pupils in corridors whispered. Though no pupil in this leafy middle-class village school was disrespectful enough to say any-thing directly to me, their comments were just about audible among the whispers. Or at least I thought I heard them.

I drove to school at the beginning of what was to be my last week. After almost ten years at the school, I had always envisaged that the last week would be a time of happy reflection. Instead my stomach was tight with anxiety. In the car, I distracted myself with the radio. On BBC Radio 4, John Humphreys of the *Today* programme was interviewing Sir Roger Singleton, the head of the Independent Safeguarding Authority (ISA). Plans were being discussed for headteachers to submit information to the ISA if they felt concerned that a teacher may have behaved improperly. I was already aware of this but had never before stopped to imagine myself as the teacher subject to scrutiny. The potential personal consequences of this new policy engulfed me. Distracted by the perceived injustice, I had forgotten that I had been accused of something and had, by telling others, indiscreetly spread my own gossip. Somewhere deep inside the minds of my colleagues, who were heterosexual, who were parents and who also lived in the surrounding countryside, this accusation may just seem feasible. My legs trembled beneath me as I continued to drive. As I turned into the school car park, I remained in the car, trying to calm down and trying to glean further information from the *Today* programme. Colleagues drew up alongside me and I stiffly stared ahead, panicking that they were listening to the same radio station and terrified that my attention to this feature was a sign of my guilt.

I had been unable to record and submit an accurate account of Mr Freeman's visit to the school, but I wondered what my headteacher had written on my file and how he would react if I asked to see it. I did not ask. I quietly left the school with a heavy heart, a snow day saving me from speeches and goodbyes. I was very sad to end my teaching career in this way.

7: A story from Canada

Derek Manson

Derek Manson currently teaches in East London, but was born and raised in rural Canada. In this chapter he explores some of the challenges he faced as a pupil in a small, traditional and conservative school community, and describes his determination that no child will ever suffer as he did at school.

From the time I was 5 years old, I knew I was different; I was as equally excited by the thought of a brand new Hot Wheels car as I was playing with my cousin's Barbie, the one with the gorgeous gold shoes. I enjoyed the company of girls, playing with them at break times and generally just following them around. On the whole I didn't act like the other boys in my class – I was more sensitive and gentle – though I didn't mind a rough-and-tumble match with them. I was me, at home, at school and in my small rural town... and it got people talking.

When I first started school I was the typical clueless youngster, who wanted to meet new friends and explore what the world had to offer. I was a bit of a trouble-maker, as I enjoyed following my own rules and doing my own 'learning'. As I continued through primary school, I was often accosted by the same insults:

'You're a girl, nah nah!'
'You probably wear dresses at home.'
'Why don't you go and play with some Barbies.'

These didn't faze me, at least at first, as I was me and I didn't mind it. As I entered Grade 4 at the age of 9, I began to recognise the typical gender stereotypes that the world portrayed all around me: boys don't cry, boys play rough, men like girls... the usual. However, these 'facts' were magnified by the conservative and rural nature of the place in which I lived.

My hometown was a rural, conservative, predominantly Christian and white place, where most men made a living through agriculture (my father included). My father was raised with the ideals that men work and women stay at home. His friends were also raised that way, which meant that their offspring – my peers – were likewise instilled with the same values and beliefs.

So as I was saying, when I got into Grade 4 I was made painfully aware that I was different, and it really began to concern me. Some of the boys would deny me access to their games and poke fun at me at every chance they had. It got me down, and my negative emotions began to skew my view of reality. Unfortunately, my teachers didn't help. I'm not saying they were bad teachers – not at all – but they subscribed to beliefs and values of our rural area. They taught to the 'stereotypes' and were always passing off what the others said to me as 'boys will be boys'. (I hate that saying when used in contexts such as this.)

When I reached middle school, I began to feel very much different about myself. I wasn't attracted to girls (though I had many female friends); I enjoyed sports but was not as athletic as the others in my class (which was an important consideration for popularity in my school). My interests and priorities led me to a fork in the road; my male peers went one way and I went the other. As gender-appropriate behaviour became ever more important to them, as it began to dovetail into their pursuit of the opposite sex, my teachers seemed to commit to the importance of gender stereotypes almost as much as my peers. I had many male teachers who would criticise anyone who transgressed the unspoken gender-identity rules:

'You're playing like a girl.'
'Come on now! What sissy throw was that?'
'Why are you wearing pink?'

As I continued to develop, my feelings, thoughts and interests began to betray me more and more. I became the target for others (mostly other boys) who wanted to have an easy laugh at my expense. By the time I reached the end of middle school, I had become withdrawn and kept only to myself and my closest friends. I had also realised that the provocations based on my differences were probably true.

When I was 15, I told my first person that I was gay. I felt such a wave of relief come over me as saying it released the pressure that had been building inside me. It was also the time that my education made me feel the most alone. We had a 'current events' session in our class one day and I brought in the news that Saskatchewan (my province) was the first province that had legalised gay marriage (in November 2004). I was ecstatic; after all the stereotypes I had grown up to believe in and all the hatred spewed from the religious people in my rural town about homosexuality, I could not believe that I had a chance at a life like others. However, my excitement came crashing down hard, as my classmates groaned and even my teacher smirked at me. I was crushed! How could so much hatred be evident in my life, especially in my school – the very place that was supposed to encourage my development into a fully functioning adult?

I continued through high school, hearing the same insults constantly hurled in my direction:

'Homo!'
'Faggot!'
'Go suck a dick, fag!'
'Stop staring at me as I'm changing, perv!'

All of this made my coming out take longer than I ever wanted it to, and longer than it should have ever taken. To make matters worse, many of the male teachers in my school would join in to an extent. The constant quips, the accusations of 'girly' traits and the laughs from teachers at the abuse thrown by others were enough to ensure my trust in educational authorities disappeared.

It was not until my final year in school that I decided enough was enough. I am me and I wanted others to know that. I started behaving more confidently, and was able to push the vitriol to the side with quick humour and harsh accusations of my own. However, I also had one saving grace: my Grade 12 English teacher. She was a woman who saw the best in everyone, able to pull out the best features of the young people in her classes and make them shine brightly like a neon sign. She recognised my sensitivity, my creativity and my femininity, and the relationship of these to my masculinity. Through her constant support and nurturing, she taught me how to be myself and, crucially, how to live by my truth. I didn't fully realise the impact her support had until I came out to her in an essay I wrote for my Grade 12 English test.

I can proudly say that thanks in huge part to an excellent teacher, I have continued to grow into my LGBT identity and my educational identity. I have vowed to ensure all children that come into my care know that *they are enough*, no matter how they behave or what they believe. My years of uncertainty and emotional degradation have helped to shape me into the man I am today: a teacher in whose classroom all are included and where difference is celebrated; and most of all, a proud gay man.

Advice for an LGBT inclusive school from Derek Manson

Listen to the LGBT voices in your school, be they teachers, parents or children. They are the ones who are living with an LGBT identity and their voices deserve to be heard and listened to. Your school will be more inclusive as a result.

8: Learning to be myself
Sarah Carroll

In this chapter, Sarah Carroll – a teacher in Cambridgeshire and a mentor on the Courageous Leaders programme – shares her story. Sarah examines how she found the courage to come out at school, and considers the responsibility we have to our students to be our authentic selves and celebrate diversity.

Of all the challenges that I thought came with teaching – workload, pay, classroom behaviour, scrutiny, etc. – I didn't think that who I was attracted to would affect my feelings about my job. I came out as gay during my first year at university, and decided on a career in teaching towards the end of my degree. I naively didn't think of the complexities that being an LGBTQ+ teacher would include, as my time at university was a liberating and primarily inclusive experience. There were so many people at university that it felt very easy to find a group of friends who I felt comfortable around.

I didn't realise the impact that feeling accepted and settled would have on me, until I felt the need to hide parts of my identity in certain situations. I didn't realise that 'coming out' wasn't a one-time thing, or why having a heightened sense of cautiousness becomes second nature after a while.

During my teacher training year, and on various secondary-school placements, I quickly noticed how my colleagues in heterosexual relationships would casually mention their partner's pronouns without thinking twice. I felt guilty that I didn't feel able to be transparent while talking about my partner. I didn't think it would bother me, but it did. I quickly realised that my career choice meant meeting hundreds of new people, staff and students, in multiple settings and situations. With every new face came a feeling of caution. Did I feel comfortable coming out to each of them? I began to feel uneasy in case they asked me about even the most trivial of things, like what I was doing at the weekend or with whom.

I quickly learned that using gender-neutral pronouns for my partner meant I felt safe from being thought of differently. I didn't want people to change their views of me. I felt annoyed about having these feelings, but I didn't like being the centre of attention all the time, as I hadn't been out for long before wanting to go into teaching. Every time I used 'they' or 'them' to describe my then girlfriend, I felt like I was lying to my work colleagues, and I didn't like that feeling. I started to feel it was unprofessional to mention my private life, and, looking back now, this adversely influenced my time starting out as a teacher.

After my teacher training, I completed my newly qualified teacher year in a secondary school that had half a dozen LGBTQ+ staff. This was a temporary maternity cover post. Feeling part of a group where I could be more 'me', where I could be a comfortable and confident teacher, was making me feel like a better teacher. Not having to second guess what I said in the staffroom or the office, and going out after work with my colleagues, really helped with my confidence levels. I was a little anxious when it became time to move schools. I worried that I wouldn't be able to replicate the feeling of belonging with my new place of work.

I needn't have worried. I've been in my current teaching position for six years now, and it was only a temporary position when I applied for it. I quickly knew I wanted to stay permanently, and was really lucky to have such a supportive head of department, who helped me to find a permanent position. Feeling settled in my place of work made me want to work harder, and feeling included in a community made me want to stay. I feel it's important to not settle for less, and I feel lucky to be where I am. I also feel a sense of duty to be visible as an LGBTQ+ teacher, because I didn't have that when I was at school. Back then, I wasn't able to articulate how I felt, but knowing that I had a visible role model would have definitely helped. Knowing that two people of the same sex could be in a relationship would have made me realise that part of who I am more quickly, and would have avoided the abundance of confusion and self-doubt that inevitably clouded my own education.

I now understand about Section 28: the law that was enforced the year that I was born, which meant that teachers and educational establishments were forbidden to teach or discuss any issues that were deemed to 'promote' anything other than traditional family values of heterosexuality. I teach about this now in a unit on equality and diversity. I feel it's really important for all students to appreciate the struggles that minority groups have encountered, and how far there still is to go. The protests against the use of the 'No Outsiders' programme in Birmingham primary schools highlights this issue. I feel privileged to be able to discuss such topics with the next generation, as I was not able to learn about such things during my time at school.

The new relationships, health and sex education framework is a positive step in ensuring that all students discuss the idea of different relationships. It is a concern, however, that some parents believe that talking about anything other than heterosexual relationships somehow 'sexualises' children. That talking about different family units with two mums or two dads isn't appropriate. These ideas need to be discussed and corrected, but I hope that as I progress through my career, the students who I teach will have by the age of 16 a better understanding of the diverse world they live in than I had at their age.

Throughout my career, I have talked to other teachers about equality and diversity issues and in particular issues surrounding LGBTQ+ identity. Some have expressed concern that they may say the wrong thing or accidentally offend others, so they avoid mentioning it altogether. This is very damaging but unfortunately all too common, as compulsory equality and diversity training is not required in the teaching profession. Other public sectors such as the police force and NHS have compulsory training in this area, and quite rightly so. It is so frustrating that teachers, who engage with thousands of children, young people, parents and colleagues over the course of their careers, are not expected to have such training as standard. Young people have questions that any teacher should have the ability and obligation to answer confidently.

It is encouraging to find that the students I teach are, overall, open-minded and tolerant of differences. They are curious and ask so many questions about things that they hear in the news, online or from their friends. I believe that as teachers, we have a responsibility to be open and encourage discussions about differences in the world, but we can only do this if we have the skills and knowledge in such areas, and if we feel supported to be our authentic selves in our places of work.

Advice for an LGBTQ+ inclusive school from Sarah Carroll

Don't assume that all staff members you work with are straight. For members of staff who identify as bisexual, just because they've dated a man in the past doesn't necessarily mean that their next partner will be male as well. Not using gender-specific pronouns in questions like 'Oh your partner? What's his name?' when talking to female colleagues will (in my experience) help with staff inclusivity. Follow the lead of the person you are talking to and listen to how they refer to their partner. If they say 'partner', try to use gender-neutral pronouns like 'they' and 'them', as this will cover most bases (including if they have a partner who defines as non-binary). If a member of staff uses 'they' or 'them' to refer to their partner, it could also mean that they are not yet comfortable in letting you know that their partner is the same sex as them. Taking the time and care to listen to whether a colleague refers to their partner as 'him', 'her' or 'they' speaks volumes for the ethos and values of that person and their place of work.

9: The role for straight allies
Donna Walsh

Donna Walsh is one of the leaders of the Courageous Leaders programme. She identifies as heterosexual and cisgendered. In this chapter, Donna explores her own experience growing up in Ireland, before reflecting on her unique role as an ally to the Courageous Leaders group.

Be yourself; everyone else is already taken. (Oscar Wilde)

I was born and raised in Ireland in the 1980s and 90s. This meant I grew up in a period of history where homosexuality was illegal, but the long road to LGBT rights in Ireland was turning a corner. In 1993, Mary Robinson, our first female president, signed into law the bill decriminalising homosexual acts, and nearly two decades later the first same-sex couple married.

In 2015, Ireland became the first country in the world to make same-sex marriage legal by popular vote. The same-sex marriage referendum and the Gender Recognition Act were both signed into law that year.

Ireland was certainly slow to emerge from a conservative outlook, restrained by the regressive elements of our society and our religion. However, mainstream Irish voters understood what was at stake and respect prevailed. The younger generations have mostly grown up with a healthy outlook, and Leo Varadkar (the Taoiseach, Ireland's political leader) is openly gay. The proverb 'it takes a village to raise a child' – meaning that an entire community must interact with children for those children to grow up in and experience a safe and healthy environment – has largely replaced the well-worn trope of 'the only gay in the village'.

Despite positive steps such as the legalisation of same-sex marriage, prejudice and discrimination against the LGBT community still abound in the UK. Take for example the disruption over the announcement of the relationships, health and sex education framework. The introduction of mandatory RSE in the UK from September 2020 should at last mean that a generation of schoolchildren will grow up knowing that 'love wins' and 'it's ok to be gay'. But some parents have expressed opposing views and targeted schools that are introducing these subjects. School leaders will be forced to acknowledge the possible issues they risk facing by introducing RSE, but are advised to establish open and constructive relationships with parents early on regarding the curriculum changes and developments.

I joined the fourth Courageous Leaders cohort in 2018. As a senior leader in a multi-academy trust, I felt responsible for driving change in school improvement. On the first face-to-face day on the programme, I stood in a university lecture room in London and nervously introduced myself to a room full of LGBT aspiring educational leaders as a straight, cisgender female. Imposter syndrome threatened my usually confident self. I felt a stark realisation of what it must be like for LGBT teachers in staffrooms and schools across the nation when faced with the situation of coming out. However, I also felt strongly that I did have a place there. I had a professional duty in my role as a school leader who believes in the importance of equality and diversity in our twenty-first century classrooms.

During the Courageous Leaders programme, 'spin the bottle' scenario discussions opened my eyes to the need for school leaders to stand up as straight allies. I was saddened by hearing stories of harassment and bullying that LGBT teachers have endured in schools through disrespect and ignorance. School leaders must recognise and support equal civil rights, gender equality and LGBT social movements. We must challenge homophobia, biphobia and transphobia in our schools, and teach our students to do the same. Our LGBT teachers should feel happy, safe and satisfied in their jobs, receiving the same respect we would expect for staff who don't identity as LGBT.

As a result of my involvement in the Courageous Leaders programme, I participated in workshops with The Kite Trust (an LGBT charity for young people and their families). These workshops introduced unfamiliar terminology and reminded me of the importance of ensuring teacher training and CPD are up to date, to help develop teachers' professional commitment to inclusivity. A lack of knowledge and training is often cited by classroom teachers as the biggest reason for inappropriate handling of homophobic, biphobic and transphobic bullying issues.

In my current school role I lead on initial teacher education (ITE), and have invested in embedding RSE education into our ITE training. I continue to actively promote and encourage the importance of the role of heterosexual allies in creating LGBT friendly workplaces and school classrooms. Straight allies can be key in transforming workplace experiences and advancing the culture of organisations. Allies who champion diversity in our schools can help to make this a reality.

I learned so much throughout that first experience of Courageous Leaders. I dissected new terminology and my own use of language; I listened to stories of prejudice I couldn't believe were happening to the teachers in our public service system. I aspired to know more and to stand side-by-side with these professionals, but most importantly I aspired to be a straight ally, promoting and encouraging other straight allies to 'come out' in support of LGBT colleagues.

Advice for an LGBT inclusive school from Donna Walsh

- Commit to actively developing your own knowledge around contemporary LGBT issues.
- Seek to create and sustain a school environment that welcomes diversity, supports equality and encourages peers to be themselves.
- Review the code of conduct and school policies to ensure they confirm the school's commitment to LGBT inclusion and equality.
- Prioritise RSE training for all teachers and support staff to equip them with the knowledge, skills and confidence they need to deliver informed lessons and facilitate open, inclusive discussions.
- Demonstrate strong leadership to promote and defend an inclusive school environment, ensuring it is core to the school's ethos.

10: Learning to address fear
Jerome Cargill

In this chapter, we return to Jerome Cargill, who considers his experience as a leader of CPD for teachers in New Zealand. As part of the Post Primary Teachers' Association, Jerome was a member of the Rainbow Taskforce, working with teachers to encourage greater LGBT inclusion in New Zealand's schools. Here Jerome reflects on some of the challenges of trying to affect positive change as an outsider, while acknowledging the fear of change and his own fear as a queer visitor to each of the schools.

Gathering together staff for weekly professional development is a conventional slot in any school calendar. Usually a member of the leadership team will be speaking to staff, sharing information about a new pedagogy focus, promoting a discussion or activity, or sharing yet another initiative that needs to be slotted somewhere into our existing practice. Occasionally these after-school presentations contain valuable information or some useful time to reflect and develop, but the majority of them provoke grumblings and frustration over their blatant sense of box-ticking or patronising tone. In the schools I've worked at, there is an immovable undertone of resentment for these meetings.

Occasionally, after-school presentations are conducted by an external speaker. The outside speaker will inevitably tell you that you are brilliant despite not having a clue who you are; they'll make you talk to the person next to you, and share a PowerPoint that contains pie charts and graphs that flick past you in a blur.

There is of course the potential for the external speaker to provoke the same grumblings and frustration; however, an external speaker also has the potential to offer freshness. Their perspective can be unique, challenging and engaging. It can shake up assumptions and promote critical thought and reflection. New ideas coming from a new point of view can be powerful, and it can be an exciting prospect.

In 2015, as a fresh-faced 26-year-old, I had my first experience of being an external speaker in a school. It was the first of many occasions where I went into schools that were alien to me to talk to staff about LGBTI+ matters. It is my journey of doing these presentations that is the subject of this chapter.

I've been fortunate to have had many opportunities to run professional development sessions on gender and sexuality, as well as undertaking research into how to trigger positive change in a teacher's practice. My perspective here is based on my personal experience, but I hope it might be transferable to other contexts where similar challenges are encountered.

Teachers are incredible people. The people working in this profession on the whole have a huge level of empathy and care for others. Based on my experiences, I am certain that teachers are listening and that attitudes are changing towards sexuality and gender identity.

I got involved in actively driving change when I applied to be part of the Post Primary Teachers' Association (PPTA) Rainbow Taskforce. The PPTA is New Zealand's teachers' union. When I was part of it, the Rainbow Taskforce was a group of six appointed teachers who represented the union on LGBTI+ matters, and who were responsible for writing an important document titled *Affirming diversity of sexualities and gender identities in the school community: guidelines for principals, boards of trustees and teachers.* As the group became established and looked for the best place to make an impact, it developed a 'Safer schools for all' workshop that was offered to schools in New Zealand for free, paid for by the teaching union in order to fill a gaping hole in the availability of professional development.

The 'Safer schools for all' presentation was in three parts. The first covered sexuality and gender 101; in other words, it introduced key terms and definitions while establishing some of the reasons why the focus of the presentation was so important. The second part shared statistics sourced from a dataset called the Youth2000 series (Clark et al., 2013). Since 2002, every five or so years, the Adolescent Health Research Group in New Zealand has surveyed 8000 teenagers about a wide range of issues. In 2015, the data revealed that students of a sexual minority were three times more likely to be bullied weekly than their heterosexual peers. It also showed that students attracted to more than one gender were four times more likely to have significant depressive symptoms than their heterosexual peers, and transgender students were five times more likely to attempt suicide than their cisgender peers. These statistics are not remarkable; they are very similar to those in the UK, the USA and in Australia. The third part of the presentation looked at the professional practice of teachers and how we might change our practice in the classroom, curriculum and school culture to be more inclusive.

I delivered the presentation several times, but I questioned how effective my early efforts were. Initially I think I painted a picture of doom and gloom when it comes to the LGBTI+ community. The examination of statistics and the familiarity of the scenarios created for me (and no doubt for the teachers listening) a myriad of emotions including sadness, guilt and despair. These emotions can be difficult to navigate when you are being asked simultaneously to reflect and to consider changes to your professional practice.

I searched for a more effective way of doing the presentation, aware that there was certainly room for improvement. I learned a lot from each effort as I adjusted my tone and approach to it. What I learned was that even in schools that are getting it significantly wrong, the focus needs to be on recognising and celebrating the queer community, including the students in our classes. Inspiring a sense of optimism was a far more effective way of enabling teachers to make changes to their practice. Focusing too much on the negatives can create a feeling of hopelessness, rather than enabling individual accountability. If presented warmly and with a focus on young people, more teachers appear to get on board with the call to action.

I also learned a lot about the power of coming out. In particular, I learned to hold off talking about myself until I was at least halfway through the presentation. I started to tell my coming out story after sharing the horrific statistics. It was effective because it helped to generate the optimism I sought. I shared my story about how at school I was represented in a lot of the negative statistics, before balancing this out with who I am now.

I worked hard to avoid painting a picture that it always *gets* better, but I found it important for teachers to believe that it can *get* better. Sharing some of my personal story helped to create that tone of warmth, by sharing some of my vulnerability.

Another key moment for the teachers hearing this presentation was learning that coming out is not a one-time thing. I remember vividly how teachers responded to this. The assumption that coming out is something that you get over and done with once is wrong, and correcting this helps teachers to understand why the conditions of their classrooms and schools need to be inclusive not just for 'pink shirt day' or 'pride week', but all the time.

I am still conflicted about the question of who is in charge of the emotional safety of the staffroom. I need to acknowledge that while every session was successful overall, there is a long list of moments that I could have navigated better. Most of these have to do with emotional safety and the way some people at times expressed ideas or experiences in discussions that were direct challenges to the messages being delivered. As the presenter, I was responsible for the immediate reaction to any contribution, but the rules of engagement were usually outside of my control. The leadership team in a school is largely in charge of setting the tone and conditions of the staffroom, and as a visitor I had to fit into this ethos and each school's established practices. On reflection, some responses to the presentation said less about attitudes towards LGBTI+ issues, and more about other issues related to the school climate that were well beyond the scope of the presentation. However, it is difficult enough to manage the emotional safety of the participants through the presentation, yet alone navigate the unique context and circumstances of the school the presentation is being delivered in.

I found it difficult to challenge the homophobic or heteronormative responses to discussion prompts, and often did not feel strong enough to combat the issues being raised. One such moment in the presentation considered how to respond to a student using the word 'gay' as a pejorative, for example by responding to being set a piece of homework with the words 'that's so gay'. In response to this prompt, teachers frequently offered a range of strong suggestions that clearly labelled this use of language as wrong, but several did not go far enough or responded in a way that almost helped to encourage the expression. Sarcastic retorts were suggested by some and the use of humour favoured by others. I still question how to best tackle these situations when they arise in a professional development setting. I'm also not sure how to engage the teachers who perhaps need the most support of all but are least likely to offer their thoughts, sitting in the quiet, reticent and reluctant corners of the staffroom.

My experiences delivering the 'Safer schools for all' workshop provoked a lot of personal reflection around how greater positive change can be achieved. Feedback on the presentation was consistently strong, but as a visitor to each school, it was difficult to know how much changed as a result of my input. The question of what actually triggers significant change is still an important one to ask, and I'm sure this trigger differs between schools.

In 2017 I was fortunate to be part of a research programme with CORE Education in New Zealand. This fellowship programme was structured to support an action-research inquiry. I set out to investigate the triggers that shift teachers' practices towards greater inclusivity for LGBTI+ students (Cargill, 2018).

To undertake this project I worked with a focus group of colleagues, spending an hour with them every fortnight. In these sessions we talked about their historical understandings of sexual and gender identity, the changes they had made in their own schools, and I introduced provocations such as articles, readings or scenarios. I collated the stories and ideas they shared and found themes emerging as we went along.

Two findings from this research helped my understanding of why teachers change their practices. The first was unsurprising and was a strong, consistent theme across all the stories that the teachers in the study had shared. It was visibility. The teachers all reflected that they could not meet the needs of students if they didn't know those needs existed. For more experienced teachers, they recalled not being aware of transgender identities early on in their careers and coming across this understanding through the media. Visibility is key to action.

My own journey has been heavily influenced by this. When I started teaching in 2009, I had never considered the implications of teaching a transgender student, nor met anyone who used gender-neutral pronouns. I wasn't meeting this need, because it just wasn't something I was conscious of. Similarly, a teacher in the study spoke of being struck during their own teacher training by the idea that not everyone in their health class might be heterosexual. They acknowledged the ridiculousness of this, but it is reflective of how normalised ideas of heterosexuality and binary gender identities are.

The 'Safer schools for all' presentations were an important vehicle for increasing visibility. One of the first activities in the presentation was to identify what LGBTI+ stands for. In every school, there was at least one group of teachers that had no ideas beyond the first two letters of the acronym.

One teacher that was part of my research project spent most of their career teaching in the UK before coming to New Zealand. They taught during Section 28, which prescribed that teachers shall not 'promote the teaching … of the acceptability of homosexuality as a pretended family relationship'. They reflected on the silencing impact this legislation had even after it was repealed in 2003. Erasure of diverse identities, homophobia and transphobia had become acceptable practices, and this did not change the day after the law was repealed. In fact Section 28 was repealed to no great fanfare and many teachers remained unaware for years that this sanction had been lifted. This teacher reflected on how sexuality and gender diversity became slowly more visible and talked about after Section 28, but they were largely shrouded in negative terms for many years after.

A further theme that emerged from the discussions on visibility was how sexuality and gender diversity are not always visible. When supporting teachers to be inclusive, we need to be sensitive to differences we might not be able to see or that might not always present themselves. For example, students might not be out yet, or they may have an LGBTI+ family member rather than being LGBTI+ themselves. Few of us would describe ourselves as truly average, and it is good practice to assume diversity – not only to support our diverse students, but also to help disrupt assumptions and to support heterosexual and cisgender students to be more aware of differences in the identities of others.

The second main finding that arose from my research project with teachers was unexpected, and opened up my thinking about making changes in teacher practice. I learned that fear is a significant barrier to being inclusive. In fact, fear is behind much of the reluctance of teachers to change.

The teachers in my study spoke at various times of the fear of getting things wrong, of using the wrong language, of using incorrect labels or of accidentally offending people by falling back on traditional assumptions. I related to this through similar feelings I have had when in a room of people who have far more diverse identities than myself. As a cisgender gay man, I often fear using incorrect pronouns, for example. But while I am trying to learn to be better at listening and being open to correction, some might withdraw completely from these situations and resist topics or dialogue where they do not feel safe. For a teacher in an English class, for instance, this might mean avoiding a discussion about AIDS that is prompted by a novel being studied. Fear of saying the wrong thing, of perpetuating stigmas, or not having the right answers might mean this important conversation is skipped over or omitted entirely. I know I did this myself before I was comfortable being out in the classroom.

Fear is what keeps us in our comfort zone as teachers. So much of our school-day structures are put in place to ensure consistency; they enable us to thrive in the comfort zone. When routines or our practice undergo significant change, it is initially very uncomfortable for some. This might go some way to explaining the reluctance to change, and I believe also explains why schools and the professionals within them experience a form of diversity inertia. Diversity inertia is the intersection of the pressure between all the reasons to change, and all the reasons not to change. We want to do better for our diverse students and be more inclusive of minority sexualities and gender identities. We hear the students that are telling us things should be different and recognise the importance of wellbeing initiatives that focus on inclusion. But on the other hand, the desire to stay in our comfort zones, the pressures of time, and the various competing priorities that fight for our energy as teachers, often means our shifts are small, temporary and not embedded in the long-term. This was a clear theme from the research with my colleagues, and I think representative of the general slow pace of change in wider education practices. Change requires bravery and courage. Perhaps these are traits we do not value and promote enough in the teaching profession.

The 'Safer schools for all' professional development was a call to action through bravery and courage, and a challenge to overcome the fear that acts as a barrier. When I started delivering the workshops I was quite dismissive of fear as being a barrier to action, but having reflected on it after seeing it manifest itself in session after session, I am now more conscious of the need to address it in a targeted and respectful manner.

Teachers need to get more comfortable with feeling uncomfortable. Young people hold more and more knowledge about sexuality and gender diversity, and we need to be open to listening to them and accept being challenged by them. It is not our job to be experts on sexuality or gender identity and it is alright for us to make mistakes, misuse language, and experience discomfort in the pursuit of a more open dialogue and safer spaces in our classrooms. The alternative is a continuation of the harm represented in the aforementioned statistics.

When I was giving those presentations, I often acted to ensure the comfort of myself and others. I now reflect on the opportunities I missed to really challenge assumptions and create more meaningful change.

It is imperative that continuing professional development on diversity and inclusion explicitly addresses sexuality and gender diversity in order to increase visibility and to combat the inertia around change. There is a systemic diversity inertia in our schools that needs to be first recognised and then conquered, empowering teachers to address their fears head on.

Advice for an LGBTI+ inclusive school from Jerome Cargill

Create safe spaces in continuing professional development (CPD) for training that specifically addresses sexuality and gender diversity.

When leading CPD, be courageous enough to challenge people, even if this is uncomfortable for those involved. Only by having challenging conversations about sexuality and gender in schools can we increase the visibility of LGBTI+ students and staff, and create a more inclusive environment for everyone.

REFERENCES

Cargill, J. (2018) *Creating safe spaces: triggering the shift for sexuality and gender inclusive classrooms.* Christchurch: CORE Education.

11: From the outside looking in: a youth leader's perspective
Jesse Ashman

In this chapter, Jesse Ashman reflects on schools from his own perspective as a queer or gender non-conforming youth leader and trainer of leaders. He explores authority and the power structures that exist within schools, and what it means to subvert this authority. In this chapter, Jesse argues that our effectiveness as school leaders should be judged on our ability to nurture young people to be self-reflective, critical thinkers who are able to express themselves in the most honest and authentic way possible. Jesse says that although Section 28 doesn't exist anymore, heteronormativity and cisnormativity are still alive and well in schools.

I believe it's important to say that I've written this chapter for a certain type of queer person; one like myself, who has no desire to live my life within the confines of homonormativity (the idea that queer people are just like straight people, and will adhere to the life and social expectations of straight people). Many LGBT people are not just like everyone else, nor would they want to be. Conforming to some or all social rules does not in any way detract from our validity as an LGBT or queer person, but our experience with leadership, authority and power may be contrary to that of our heterosexual and cisgendered peers.

I currently work with senior LGBT leaders from across the business sector and many (but not all) of them are different to me and most of the queer people I spend my time with. They conform to certain ideals of gender and sexual normativity. In this chapter, I'm concerned with how to people like me can step up as leaders and how this encompasses rule-breaking in a broader sense.

Gender non-conformity

Out of all the identity labels, the one that most sticks with me is 'gender non-conforming', as it defines itself with specific reference to resistance to conformity. It's one that is sometimes used specifically to refer to children, but it's also the one I find most useful when speaking to groups who have a limited knowledge of LGBT identities. It's the sort of term that explains itself – if you have a concept of what gender is (and despite Butler's best efforts, most of us do), then you can form a concept of what 'gender non-conforming' looks like without any additional information. I've found 'gender non-conforming' is one of the best terms to use to begin to set your own rules within a space. The parameters of this identity are set by resisting what is expected, and it will move situationally as those expectations shift.

To be a gender non-conforming leader is complex. A leader is someone who is expected to be followed; and to be non-conformist, and a leader at the same time, is to take a radical approach to the nurturing of individuality and to the power of critical thinking and self-reflectiveness within each participant of a group. This applies to classroom groups just as much, if not most of all, as it does to any other type of group.

To give a little more context for what I mean by this type of non-conformity: I was brought up believing that half the world are women and half the world are men. Of those women and men, half are straight and half are gay. This was a fairly radical idea to bring up a child with; that both sexual orientation and gender are randomly determined with equal chance of either outcome. This is, of course, completely untrue and speaks to a now outdated binary notion of both sex and gender.

Growing up as someone who is transgender, bisexual, polyamorous, and who has dyslexia and a sensory processing disorder (all things I didn't learn were applicable to me until I was an adult), the wrongness of this view of the world was extremely apparent to me; the way I experienced the classroom, gender and the world was completely at odds with even the fairly radical upbringing I had. For better or worse, this has made me always feel the need to question set assumptions, authority and rules given. If it weren't for my extreme fear of being shouted at (sensory processing disorder) I would perhaps have been a rule-breaker in the more traditional sense in the classroom environment. As it was, it was mainly gender rules and gender non-conformity that were my avenue for expressing dissatisfaction with the status quo. How then could going into adulthood and taking on a role as a leader be reconciled with non-conformity as an identity?

Rules

When I was in school, I had wanted to become a teacher not because of a deep-set commitment to knowledge, learning or even schools in general, but instead because of a thirst for power that was not afforded to me in the school system. Rules were set by teachers and flagrantly broken by pupils; reporting any misdeeds to the teacher was in itself a misdeed of 'telling tales'. As a child, it seemed to me that what the school system really needed was a true authoritarian – why set so many rules if you weren't going to stick to them?

And beyond the rules, why set a reward system that seems to have one mechanism for some members of the class and a completely different one for others? Why does a pupil who is extremely loud most of the time receive a sticker for being quiet for half an hour, but I, who am usually quiet (unless speaking up about how other people are wrong), receive no such sticker for all my collective half-hours of quietness? Both these game mechanics of the classroom suggested one clear path to receiving the greatest sticker bounty: get caught breaking rules intermittently and reap stickers when observed merely abiding by the most basic classroom rules. If only there had been some true authority in the classroom, such a loophole in the system wouldn't have existed and I would have had a full sticker book.

You might be thankful that I did not, in fact, become a teacher. Preoccupied with the notion of power, I perversely graduated wanting to become a police officer, but quickly let go of that idea on learning that I may need to chase criminals. As I moved through the school system, my frustration with the behaviour of authority didn't lessen but instead stewed into a long-standing resentment of the school system, its ethics and many of the practitioners within it. What I became instead was a youth worker – an occupation I am sure I wouldn't have chosen if I wasn't a queer person.

I eventually became a youth leader. As a young person, I had attended a trans youth group. which was my first introduction to radical youth work, group decision-making, and more broadly to the idea of valuing self-expression and non-conformity in an environment outside of the family home. I was extremely lucky that the radical values I had were mirrored by my family; so much so that when I transitioned, my father was disappointed because he thought that I would not identify as queer anymore.

For many young people, the classroom is the first true power structure they encounter, and a teacher is the first leader they encounter that has not gained that power through family ties. For most young people, the classroom is the first structure we're coercively forced into by the state education system – it's our first interaction with state power, with rules and with large groups of other children. It's also often the first interaction with the idea of rules and punishment that doesn't come from a clear place of love (as, if we're lucky, it does from a parent or carer). With this in mind, our presence in this system as LGBT people is one of power and vulnerability.

Subversion

As LGBT people, we're often defined by how we subvert rules put upon us by authority, whether that be from heteronormativity (the assumption that everyone is straight), cisnormativity (the assumption that not only is everyone straight, but that everyone is cis – that is, not transgender), or more recently, homonormativity. For myself, this is something I felt acutely at school – the way I expressed myself in terms of gender was very much not allowed within the rules, and neither were the people I was attracted to. This bled into other areas of difference as well, in a way that can't be pinned down to either sexual orientation, gender or neurodivergence. For example, teachers would often attempt to brush hair out of my face as I had long, messy, frizzy hair for a large chunk of my school life. This is something that I categorically hatedThe teachers disguised their unease at my long hair as breaking school rules about self-presentation and neatness, but I knew that their real concern was more to do with transgressing expectations of gender presentation.

The way authority and power is abused in leadership roles is often incidental to these assumed rules. None of the teachers who put their classes into boy/girl groups, brushed hair out of my face or told me how to sit were intentionally asserting power – and yet it was still happening. This meant that once I was put in a position of being in charge of a youth group, the last thing I wanted to be was a teacher. I wanted to be a youth leader: someone who takes on the needs and characteristics of the group to guide them. When parents mistook me for one of the older boys in the group, this felt like a badge of honour – thank goodness I wasn't like all those teachers! I was still very much a young person myself, but how the group was led and how rules operated stuck with me as a lesson in how to subvert authority.

This perceived (and of course incorrect) dichotomy between being a teacher and a true leader mirrors and encompasses a notion we're often tempted to accept within the LGBT community – that being queer and having power over others or being in charge do not and cannot go together. Most LGBT people who work with young people have experienced at least one instance of homophobia, biphobia or transphobia being leveraged to try to subvert the authority of the teacher or responsible adult. For me this happened in my first placement, where the second-most popular question to ask me (after 'Can I go to the toilet?') was, 'Are you a boy or a girl?' This same question had followed me through years and years of trauma, and seemed to reinforce that being a queer person and being a leader (as opposed to just being the person put in charge, whether or not that garners any authority) is not something that is possible.

This is true up to a point; under the current power structures we have in place, being anything that doesn't fit the assumed rules of society is somewhere irreconcilable. The curriculum is set by non-LGBT people (it didn't include us until recently, and still doesn't in some areas), as are the laws (Section 28, the ban on giving blood, the spousal veto, etc.), as are the much more nuanced codes of acceptability (sitting like a girl, pink for girls, blue for boys, boys don't cry…). To be someone who so flagrantly breaks all these modes of acceptability and then purports to uphold all the other rules creates a cognitive dissonance in young people.

It doesn't go unnoticed if a school has a gendered uniform policy but then butch Mrs X in class 9 wears trousers to class every single day. This doesn't just centre on the rules that apply specifically to gender though; when we see someone who breaks social norms in a position of leadership also seeking to uphold them, this undermines the fabric of the classroom as a one-size-fits all approach. Being quiet in class or sitting still doesn't seem quite so important now that we know the rules don't apply equally to children and adults, or that some people have an unspoken difference – one not available to young people – meaning they are allowed to break these norms. The absence of consideration for neurodiversity within our classrooms (or any group setting for that matter) goes hand in hand with the absence of consideration for gender diversity.

When working with young people, the responsible adult (youth worker, teacher, camp leader, etc.) has, of course, a certain power over the group. How this is used can fall into a hyper-conformity to the rules (for example, being strict so as to avoid any kind of negative comments from children on the topic of prescribed non-conformity) or, more authentically, to create a type of authority that comes specifically from subversion.

Towards a liberational view of authority

There are lots of instances where we can understand 'leadership' more broadly as setting the rules within any group parameter. When we think about this through the lens of non-conformity, the outlier in any group can become the leader through (intentional or non-intentional) rule-breaking. This is shown no more acutely than in the corporate world. In many companies there is a specific style of dress, manner of speaking and authority etiquette, and when a non-conforming person enters the meeting who is so blatantly and clearly breaking them, they become a leader by their mere presence. This can be any type of non-conformity, but for gender it means having a visible queerness that forces a subversion of a set of specific rules. I'm extremely lucky that all the meetings like these that I am part of are for the very purpose of speaking about LGBT inclusion – but for a youth leader or teacher in a school setting, subversion of the established rules is not the role you are expected to play, either by your employers or by your students.

So what does a more liberational view of authority look like in practice?

As a teacher or group leader, you can set the tone for young people to an extent. We had very few rules in the first youth group I ran. They broadly boiled down to:

- Be safe.
- No slurs (racial or otherwise).
- No stealing.

Added to this were any rules the young people wanted to contribute to their 'working agreement' for the session (a practice picked up from Gendered Intelligence's trans youth group). For many of the young people we worked with, this was the first time they had been given agency over a power structure, and by extension agency over a leader. Instead of becoming the law as a leader, you started to become a tool for agency. When rules are clearly explained and mutually agreed upon, we start to see the root power of leadership. Young people would start to request specific things they wanted to do in sessions, suggest parameters for activities and raise problems they were having. The 'No stealing' rule was mainly put in place after a number of young people had been found stealing food from the kitchen, including raw eggs. This rule came with the addendum 'If you are hungry, let a member of staff know.'

Every rule had a genesis like this; either someone had suggested it for a reason or it had resulted from something happening that either got us (the group) in trouble with the building staff (in the egg-theft situation), or worsened the experience for the whole group (for example, if something was broken). Having this set-up for where rules come from gives young people the space to question authority and to question arbitrary rules, as they know there is a clear thought process and accountability to each rule.

Further to this, this allows acceptance for non-conforming leaders – once only rules with reasons are allowed in a group, then there is no place for normativity to be accepted as one of the rules.

While representing the wellbeing and opinion of the group, leaders also have to hold themselves accountable. This means being as authentic as possible, or as authentic as you feel safe to be. Within most settings where you are working with young people (or any group), there will be at some point a power structure that doesn't come from you personally – either from your employer, headteacher, client, boss, line-manager, or from society at large if you work in a particularly liberated institution. The extent to which you can navigate the power structure authentically says something about your sense of agency within the institution.

Conclusion

To be a queer or gender non-conforming leader is to subvert power structures and to exist as both a subversion of authority and the authority itself. The only way out of this, for both leader and students, is to create spaces that take a radical approach to governance, where we accept that power that is not sanctioned by the group is always oppressive. Your effectiveness as a leader should never be judged on your ability to subdue a group of young people, but more on your ability to nurture young people to be self-reflective, critical thinkers who are able to express themselves in the most honest and authentic way possible. To achieve this, we have to live these values ourselves and shed the fear instilled in us from the oppressive school systems most of us grew up in. Section 28 doesn't exist anymore, but that doesn't mean that heteronormativity and cisnormativity in the classroom are gone forever – but there is a hope we can banish them from our own classrooms and groups in the future, through our authentic presence.

Advice for an LGBT inclusive school from Jesse Ashman

Look for the ways in which the environments you work in stifle non-conformity of all kinds and push back against those systems in whatever big or small ways you can. The barriers for LGBT students, families and teachers do not exist in isolation and cannot be tackled without advocating for structural change.

REFERENCES

Butler, J. (2006) *Gender Trouble*. New York: Routledge.

Stryker, S. (2008) 'Transgender history, homonormativity, and disciplinarity', *Radical History Review* 2008 (100) pp. 145–157.

12: The solo traveller sitting in your classroom
Jerome Cargill

In his final contribution to this book, Jerome Cargill presents a vignette based on his experiences as a solo traveller. He considers what it means to be an outsider in a new country, and reflects on what this can teach us about creating schools and classrooms that are welcoming and which allow our students to be their authentic selves.

From February to April in 2018, I left New Zealand to travel through Vietnam and China on my way to make a new home in London. For most of my time in Vietnam I had travel companions, but for most of China I was a solo traveller. When I was by myself I felt like an outsider at times, being the only European and English speaker in many situations. Particularly in China I found myself in environments that by their very design excluded me from participating.

While I enjoyed the extended break, I missed the classroom and pedagogy was never too far from my mind. Travelling and education are very similar in that they are both about journeys. Travelling from the south of Vietnam to the north of China could be a metaphor for a student's journey through school: it's about making sense of new environments, gaining knowledge, and achieving success. There is also the challenge of maintaining your own identity and agency in the face of systems that tend to favour homogeneity.

An important part of my identity relates to my sexuality as a gay man. It was a struggle at times to have that part of my identity validated during my trip. When buying clothes, most shop assistants attempted to sell me something for my girlfriend, and arranged marriages with local girls were proposed more than once after locals discovered I was travelling alone. In Vietnam, I spent some time in Yen Duc village, a couple of hours from Hanoi. At my homestay I had to give up trying to explain I had a male partner. At first I was laughed at, then later I was reasoned with – my homestay mother conceded, explaining through a translator, that if I only held other boys' hands and nothing more then it would be ok. This might not have necessarily been homophobia, but more of a cultural clash where my identity was not recognised by this family in Vietnam.

More overt homophobia happened later in Chengdu, when an Australian in a food tour group delighted in telling us his 'awful' story about accidentally going to a Chinese gay bar. He told us he didn't know what type of bar it was, found it was full of only men and experienced guys hitting on him. He then explained how he got out of there as quick as he could, barely concealing his disgust in his re-enactment. This form of homophobia pales in comparison to the fabulous young boy I saw being spat at in Shanghai. While that was disturbing to witness, the ubiquity of spitting in China makes me doubt how directed an attack that was. But then again there was no attempt to apologise.

In our classrooms, students may find our educational spaces similar to travelling in a foreign country.

How do we ensure we are validating our students' authentic identities? How are we ensuring that everyone feels like they belong? Are our classrooms inclusive of all the differences that our students bring? Alienation can be brought about through language barriers and cultural practices that don't find space for difference. The challenge is for educators to make our classrooms inclusive destinations for all our travellers. I think I've learned a lot from the reminder of both what it feels like to be the outsider and the privilege of experiencing this so rarely.

Advice for an LGBT inclusive school from Jerome Cargill

To create truly inclusive classrooms, teachers must make a commitment to do whatever it takes to provide each student in the community with their inalienable right to belong and to feel safe in being their authentic self.

13: Getting it right for everyone
Johnpaul McCabe

In this chapter, Johnpaul McCabe looks at the inclusion of LGBT teachers within school communities. Starting with a reflection of his own upbringing and the challenges he faced as a pupil at school, Johnpaul recommends some principles for schools that are inclusive and safe for all LGBT stakeholders. Throughout his narrative, Johnpaul argues that schools which get it right for one diverse group get it right for everybody.

In this chapter I make use of the word 'queer' both as an umbrella term for LGBT+ and for someone who self-identifies as queer. Its use addresses some of the clumsiness of the LGBT+ acronym, which itself is increasingly viewed as too rigid and reinforcing of difference. The use of 'queer' is meant as reclamation and no offense is intended. In my life and in my classroom I use the term queer interchangeably with the acronym LGBT+.

I am not the first to say that growing up in Scotland is no utopia. I wish I could say that I have lived the life I wanted and met my full potential, taking advantage of every opportunity, but that is not the truth. In the past I know I have been less myself, often not truly engaged and rarely, if ever, able to give my true self to anyone. Even now I hold back a part of myself, afraid it might make me even more 'other'. Growing up in a society that was not welcoming and was in fact shamed by anything queer has and continues to limit my true potential, both professionally but also personally.

Historically, Scotland has dragged its heels when it comes to the pursuit of equality compared to England. My students are frequently shocked to hear that homosexuality was only decriminalised in 1982, with the

Scottish government taking until 2019 to issue an apology to those who were criminalised for their love. Born in 1988, the community I grew up in – a working-class, deprived ex-council estate – was typical of much of the west of Scotland, and also typical of many places in the UK. It was a place where not liking football was blasphemous and being in 'the young team' (the local gang) was a better measure of success than academic achievement. Despite being fortunate to have a family that insisted 'if you're gay, that's ok', I grew up in a culture where 'gay' was the worst thing you could be. Before I knew much or anything about the world, I knew I couldn't be gay. That would be the end. I could not turn to those who encouraged my imagination and my ambitions, those with whom we should always be able to seek safety and sanctuary – my teachers. They were restricted under Section 28 of the Local Government Act, which meant schools could not 'promote the teaching… of the acceptability of homosexuality as a pretended family relationship'. They could certainly not tell me that it was ok to be gay.

Forever the good modern studies student (the subject I now teach), I have always been keenly interested in the news and understanding the world, both in local terms and more globally. Growing up as a teenager in the 2000s and then moving on to university, I was acutely aware of the debate about the legitimacy of same-sex relationships. Even as the privately funded referendum on the repeal of Section 28 failed, so too did the country as it legalised only civil partnerships. Same-sex relationships were real but not equal to those of mixed-sex couples, whose right to marriage it seemed was never a question for debate. It was only in 2014 that equal marriage was finally achieved, yet by 2020 there remain barriers in law to me being a fully equal member of society, to donating my blood, to becoming a father. We still debate and have protests on the streets of the UK over telling stories to children about families with two mums. This warns me and other queer teachers that it is safer and more sensible to hide. We are not getting inclusion right for queer teachers and we are not getting it right for every child.

Passionate about my curricular area, I pursued it at undergraduate level. However, as much as I considered the idea of becoming a teacher, I never felt that going back to school or becoming a teacher was a safe or healthy option. After coming out I would often ask myself how I could return to the place where I learned to police myself to such detriment. As I began to peel back the layers of internalised homophobia that I had wrapped myself in, I felt that returning to the institutions which had sowed doubt in the love my family showed me unconditionally was never going to be the right choice. In time, this fear of returning to school turned into sadness, disappointment and resentment.

At this point I find myself asking, why do you need to know all this? Well because we are now into the third decade after the millennium, we are a decade on since the 2010 Equality Act, and yet to be queer is still to be lesser. Equality of access for all does not exist, inclusion is a dream and safety is still a concern. I tell you my history because it will be the history of many others – both those who became teachers and those who didn't. If we want the best of the best in our schools, then we need to make sure that the education of the past exists only in textbooks and becomes the stories we tell about how far we have come as a society. I share with you what I have never really shared with others – I am less myself because of my experience, and so I am also less of the teacher I can be. As a result, I am not the only one to be impacted; it is also my school, my colleagues, my community and ultimately my students that are now negatively impacted by our history of prejudice towards LGBT+ people. If we get it right for staff – if we create workplaces that are inclusive of queer identities, which understand the impact of intolerance – then we can also get it right for all of our children, so that no one goes to school ashamed of who they are or who they may be.

While working for a time in the charity sector, I often met young LGBT+ people who felt excluded, lost and rejected in a country that had recently legalised same-sex marriage. They felt failed by an education system that didn't see them, and didn't recognise or validate their identity. School was not a place of inclusion, support or safety. For these young people, their identity became a barrier to getting the education they needed to be confident, successful, responsible and independent members of our society. If when describing who you are, the response you hear is 'it's a phase', 'kids will be kids', 'try to fit in more', 'we don't have gay people here', 'you're too young to know', 'you will grow out of it', 'there is nothing I can do', or 'I can't talk to you about this', is it really any surprise that your academic success and life chances become limited?

If we don't get it right for all our children – if they don't feel safe, nurtured and included, and if they are not respected – they will not be healthy, they will lack ambition, and they will not achieve. This manifests itself in different ways depending on a range of other factors, as well as the level of support and love shown to children. For some students it shows itself in subtle levels of disengagement, such as coming to school late, being quiet in some classes, and picking subjects to protect their personal safety (by avoiding other young people who are bullies) rather than based on aptitude and the love of a subject. More obvious are increased rates of truanting, refusal to attend classes with certain teachers, gaps in learning, awards not achieved and potential never met. The most visible and alarming outcomes are high levels of self-harm, substance abuse and death by suicide. All of these negative behaviours are our concerns as practitioners regardless of whether a child is LGBT+ or not, but I know from my personal and professional experiences that they are particularly symptomatic of a failure of queer children to thrive.

Creating learning communities which are open and visibly inclusive for all, including LGBT+ staff, will demonstrate to children and young people struggling that they are valued and safe. If we do not get it right for LGBT+ staff then we can never get it right for every child, and schools will continue to fail to provide the best experience for their students.

Queer or not, all of us have grown up through changes in our society and many of us have engaged in the debates on the legitimacy of LGBT+ identities, including our right to love and to live. Many in education have used prejudiced terminology and held views that would now be regarded as abhorrent. I have. This is a legacy that stays with us and one we must face up to if we are to move forward. There are those who have overcome so many hurdles to become our colleagues, and those hurdles are not simply an experience consigned to the past but instead continue almost constantly to influence their thoughts, levels of engagement and honesty.

I hope that my experience is something you will have never faced and that my perspective is something new for you to contemplate. Sadly, for many who have experienced any form of prejudice such as racism, disablism, sectarianism, bigotry and sexism, much of this will be very familiar. After five years, I still consider myself new to the teaching profession, with much to learn from more knowledgeable and experienced colleagues. What I do know is that I work in a school where I feel included, respected and safe. Having reflected on why that is the case, I hope to offer some thoughts on how my own school's approach could be replicated in other learning environments.

'Getting it right for every child' (GIRFEC) is an approach that aims to help all children and young people in Scotland to grow up feeling loved, safe and respected so they can realise their full potential. It is an approach that professionals in Scotland need to contemplate when working with children, and has been in use since 2006. There are eight factors to consider when talking about a child or young person's wellbeing. These are the SHANARRI indicators: safe, healthy, achievement, nurture, active, respect, responsibility and inclusion. By creating learning communities that are **safe** for all LGBT+ staff, we do our part in promoting positive mental and physical **health** for a community at risk of higher rates of self-harm, substance abuse, poor mental health and suicide. To get the very best out of practitioners, so that they **achieve** for themselves and for our students, we must ensure our schools are **nurturing**. In turn, we will find that practitioners are **active** in the school community as well as in the lives, hearts and memories of our learners and their families. When growing a community where LGBT+ identities are **respected** and valued, we also need to help meet the public sector **responsibility** to promote positive partnerships between all protected characteristics. Though not an easy journey, ensuring the **inclusion** of LGBT+ people will foster learning environments that better reflect the world around us and are inclusive of everyone.

Safe

In Scotland, as in the rest of the UK, a guaranteed probationary year exists for newly qualified teachers following their time at university or in postgraduate teacher training. The pathways into teaching vary in other systems. Something that is universal is that those new to the profession should know that they are safe. The fear of prejudice during my student teacher placements, probationary year and pursuit to a permanent post resulted in me being very cautious, and a lifelong default of self-oppression continued. Make it clear to all who come into your school that it is a safe working environment. Be explicit in this and ensure that any prejudice shown towards or about LGBT+ people would be treated with as much concern and urgency as if it was a racist, sexist, disablist or bigoted incident. If your school is able to make clear to temporary staff (such as student and supply teachers) that they are safe, then they can give more of themselves to the role they are there to fulfil.

Early on in our journey of creating a safe place of learning in my current school, we received push-back from a small cohort of students who produced and disseminated homophobic materials around the school. Fellow students reported and identified the culprits, and the school's pastoral team, supported by the on-site police officer, met with the students and made clear the severity of their actions. As a queer member of staff, my first response to this incident was to hide, withdraw and disengage. However, the actions of our students and staff made me feel safe and supported, and assured me that the behaviour demonstrated was being treated extremely seriously at all levels. Colleagues checked in on me and I knew that in the face of this incident I was protected. After intense engagement with these students and their parents and carers, the students began to actively engage in lessons that touched on diversity, sought a greater understanding of LGBT+ identities, and by the end some were active defendants of LGBT+ people.

A clear lesson we learned from this incident is that when faced with such prejudiced behaviours, we must address them head on, identifying ignorance and providing opportunities to learn and understand in the first instance. Making a place safe for discriminated groups does not always require an immediate sanction, but it always requires full engagement. A warning on its own is not nearly as beneficial as making a deliberate effort to address the root of the prejudiced behaviour. Don't ignore language in a corridor or classroom. Challenge it, discuss it and if need be escalate it. Set out a clear series of steps for those involved to follow when addressing the behaviour that is being displayed, so that all in the community can feel confident that they are in a safe space. I am confident that if I address any challenging behaviour in my classroom – regardless of whether it is racist, homophobic or bigoted – it will all be treated with the same level of seriousness by those more senior than me, and it is this confidence that makes me feel safe and supported in my role.

Healthy

The size and resources available to your institution will vary, but there is much that we can do to encourage a healthy workforce. We need only look at the fact that there is almost no LGBT+ representation in professional football to see that the lack of participation of openly LGBT+ people in male sport is a scandal. For many LGBT+ people, changing rooms are historically a place of vulnerability. For many in school it was and is a place where prejudiced language, away from supervising adults, is rife. That legacy continues and LGBT+ people have lower levels of participation in sport and physical activity.

In my few years in teaching I have seen that schools are often excellent at promoting the use of their sporting facilities to staff. This ranges from staff yoga to badminton or exercise classes. To address the hesitation felt by many queer people to participate in sports, there are small actions that can be taken. Make the inclusion of marginalised groups visible by putting up posters that challenge stereotypes in sport, such as images of women in traditionally male sports. Have lessons on parasport and discuss prejudice in sport. You could work with external organisations that aim to increase participation of LGBT+ people in sport to make your provision for students more inclusive. This sends a clear message to staff that your sporting spaces are safe places for everyone to be healthy.

I previously worked in the cancer care sector and we learned that marginalised groups were less likely to access the services offered. After some exploration it became clear that having experienced discrimination in the past, potential service users often choose not to access the cancer support offered for fear of that experience being repeated again. This knowledge has stayed with me since and offers lessons in supporting the mental health of all school staff.

Some institutions provide on-site mental-health support services, while others will engage an external provider or signpost staff to a range of organisations. Regardless of the level of provision available, make sure it is with a practitioner or service that is inclusive. Ask if they have experience in supporting marginalised groups. Create a staff health and wellbeing board that explicitly mentions inclusive services or uses an inclusive logo or charter mark. For many, past experiences of institutional discrimination will be an automatic barrier to access that requires that an extra step to demonstrate that this service is different.

Achieving

Recent films such as *Hidden Figures* and *Pride* offer excellent examples of groups whose contribution to key events in history and moments of progress have been excluded. In my classroom I have a growing collection of books for my students to read that highlight women who have achieved amazing things and men who dared to be different, alongside texts that are celebrations of ethnic minorities. Their presence goes unquestioned and unchallenged, and the students enjoy discovering someone new and inspirational. Outside my classroom there is a display celebrating successful people of different and multiple identities, including code-breaker Alan Turing, the mathematician and founder of modern computing. Putting up displays and actively celebrating the achievements of a range of diverse role models around your institution sends a clear message that regardless of sexual orientation, ethnicity, ability, etc. we all have the potential to achieve and to be successful.

It has been argued that such action is tokenistic, and yes on its own it might be, if it is the only step taken to celebrate diversity. However, when one person looks at such a display and recognises some of the struggles that a celebrated figure may have overcome, the display may be the difference between a positive and negative approach to their work – be they student or staff. To borrow a phrase from social media and my students, they may 'feel seen'. To be 'seen' is to feel recognised, and to know that some part of your identity has been acknowledged or become visible in a positive way. To ensure that such action is not tokenistic, take time to work on a diversity calendar for your academic year. You can start from scratch or look online. Our most recent school diversity calendar was inspired by Glasgow University and was freely accessible. Use this to set out a year-long series of events or themes to inspire action throughout. Events could be based on Black History Month, LGBT+ History Month, or celebrations like National Coming Out Day and Interfaith Week.

Have temporary displays, invite in external speakers, hold assemblies or create stakeholder engagement events. Our LGBT+ History Month events have involved staff coffee mornings and rainbow flag signing. Students have watched important films with LGBT+ themes and have even taken part in face painting. The signed flag is proudly displayed on a wall in our school's reception, and is one of the first things seen by everyone who enters our school. Each and every one of these actions allows your institution to celebrate the achievements of marginalised groups and sends a very clear message: that all in your community – staff, students, the people at home – are celebrated and welcomed, and their achievements are seen.

Nurture

All good places of work should nurture talent and ambition. My advice is to be open-minded and prepared to take chances by giving staff the opportunity to explore, trust and follow their professional judgement. It is important to listen, support and facilitate opportunities that will encourage the best in your staff, who will in turn give their best to you. When I first arrived at my school, I highlighted the experience I had coming from the equalities sector prior to teaching and I wanted to support the school's efforts to be an inclusive learning environment. This was welcomed by senior management and I was met with an open door and a listening ear. I was challenged, I was sent away to think further, I was signposted and I was guided. And today I still am. At times I was told no, or not right now – and that is ok. Education isn't a sprint, it's a marathon: a continuous cycle of reflection, learning, implementation and evaluation. The key thing throughout is that a nurturing environment is encouraged for staff as well as students.

Large parts of the Scottish education system are not hugely prescriptive and instead practitioners are guided by a series of frameworks. This means that as a teacher I have the freedom to design the curriculum I deliver to my students so long as it meets certain outcomes. For example, early in secondary school my students should identify groups that experience inequality and make suggestions to address this inequality. This gives me, and all other modern studies teachers, the flexibility to explore groups of mine and the students choosing. As a result I have developed a series of lessons that explore hate crime in our society and the responses to it. Students can then focus further on groups of their choice, such as LGBT+ people, ethnic minorities or disabled people.

I recognise that this is quite specific to the Scottish system, but it has also only been possible because of the nurturing support shown to me by my seniors. I have been entrusted as a professional to meet the needs of my students both academically and as citizens of our country. I know that in the past, inclusion of LGBT+ identities in the classroom has been met with resistance and push-back from staff, students and their people at home. By making it clear that such identities and experiences are valid and lived, we help to nurture understanding of the different protected characteristics and in time the issues become less contentious.

As a school we have worked hard to develop an inclusive curriculum. We don't have LGBT+ lessons; we have lessons on life which recognise that LGBT+ people exist. In science, when students learn about reproduction, they also learn about family diversity through surrogacy and adoption. In music, students learn about the music of Queen and the life of Freddie Mercury. Our art department will explore the work of Grayson Perry and cover topics such as mental health, equality and discrimination. While learning coding in computing, students will design a website on LGBT+ terminologies; in maths, students work out if Sam and her mums will get to the airport quicker by car or by train. The history department looks at all the victims of the Holocaust and the symbols used by the Nazis (including the pink triangle), while the English department explores barriers to transgender inclusion. In whichever system you work, there are always opportunities for staff to be empowered as change makers, to be brave and to take chances. What is important with our places of work is that they are a nurturing place where all feel part of the team.

Active

Around the UK, our educational establishments and wider workforce are at different stages on the journey towards creating a more inclusive workplace. Larger institutions have the advantage of increased numbers of professionals to help realise change, while smaller institutions benefit from greater personalisation. The important thing for all institutions is to be active and to not wait until something has happened to highlight a significant and urgent need to change. Across my region of Scotland, practitioners from all levels of healthcare, the police, social work and education (including nursery, primary, secondary, further and higher education) have been coming together to share practice on inclusion.

Our efforts to become an inclusive school and develop a curriculum more representative of marginalised groups began when a student transitioned and we needed to meet their needs. Staff in the school felt uncertain and lacked confidence on a range of issues, from the use of terminology and pronouns to tackling questions and behaviours from other students.

Our school decided to be proactive in its approach, to try to plan ahead and be as prepared as possible. As a secondary school where a single student sees a large number of teachers, we decided it was best to take a whole-school approach to support staff to be as skilled and knowledgeable as possible. With knowledge comes confidence, and in surveys our staff increasingly reported that they felt better equipped to support our LGBT+ students. The reality is that in working on inclusion for our students, we as a staff team have also become more understanding of the experience of our LGBT+ staff too. It was important to us as a school that in our pursuit to create a learning environment for all, we actively included all staff. This in turn has wider benefits where staff feel confident to be active in the school community, knowing they are part of a more engaged, respectful and supportive team.

Respect and responsibility

I am yet to come across a learning environment that would not regard respect as a key priority.

It is inevitable that with diversity there comes disagreement, but that does not have to lead to exclusion or disrespect. For my school, our journey towards creating an inclusive community for LGBT+ people involved resistance from some within our community. However, in the face of this we have learned ways to foster and promote respect between different groups. The 2010 Equality Act sets out a responsibility to promote positive relationships between all protected characteristics, and no one person's right to express their views is more important than another's right to feel respected and included.

While the focus for us at the start of our journey has been on our LGBT+ students, staff and families, it has in reality been our pathfinder to wider inclusion. We have learned more about our school, what works, the values of our students and areas that require more focus. It absolutely is a fundamental responsibility of the education sector to promote respect, and by focusing on the historically taboo communities that have a long history of discrimination, we are learning more about how we can get it right for everyone. When in the past someone at home has raised an objection to our efforts at creating an inclusive curriculum, our pastoral staff, our leadership team and our local authority have all engaged with the complainant. They have made it clear that the responsibility we as a school have to promote respect for all will continue, and they have been invited in to discuss it further. As a member of staff, knowing that the support is there in the face of complaints is empowering. It does however highlight the need to understand resistance better, and that is an important lesson I have taken away.

In the face of resistance, don't be afraid to engage or enquire further. We surveyed our staff to get a better understanding of our demographic as well as their attitudes towards LGBT+ inclusion. The survey was anonymised and some of the responses from a minority of staff were challenging. In response to this we encouraged an 'open door' policy where anyone who did have issues or questions could come, without judgement, to find out more. In one case the challenge was not that they were against inclusion, but instead they wondered why there had to be a focus on separating out the needs of LGBT+ stakeholders from that of anyone else. Through discussion and respectful engagement, the person came to understand that the ambitions of our work towards LGBT+ inclusion were the same as their wider ambitions for educational equality. The colleague began to appreciate that sometimes we have to recognise our different experiences before we can begin to eliminate the barriers that separate us. This member of staff is now one of the most vocal proponents on our journey towards inclusion and has spearheaded greater visibility in their curriculum. Encouraging respect for queer members of staff requires that that respect be extended to all, and again highlights that the approaches we take towards an LGBT+ inclusive workplace help to get it right for everyone.

Included

The release of *Black Panther* was important as it showed that films with majority black casts could be successful. A red-haired Scottish princess in *Brave* lets my very ginger niece see a strong girl to whom she can relate. I am still waiting for Disney to show me a prince who finds the man of his dreams. Sadly it might be a long wait. Visibility is important and historically marginalised groups have been (and continue to be) hidden. But the reality is that we, as educators, do not need to wait for Disney. The stories we tell, the questions we answer, and the lessons we create have the power to ensure that all children grow up in a world where they see positive representations of themselves and feel included.

In doing so we also go some way to challenging the preconceptions of the past. We create, through our lessons, spaces that are inclusive. As my niece now reads about families with two dads, I feel less these days that my right to marriage is second class. When students are comfortable

COURAGE IN THE CLASSROOM

asking after a pregnant colleague's wife, I see respect. In teaching lessons where students talk about the LGBT+ representation of members of parliament with no sense of taboo or hesitation, I feel safe. When I pop into a straight teacher's classroom to borrow glue while 14-year-old students sensitively talk about the experience of gay men in Nazi Germany, I now feel included. Equality and inclusion cannot be left to the marginalised to realise – it is a responsibility for us all.

Do make sure your policies are explicitly inclusive. We are all a product of our past experiences, and the experiences of the marginalised lead them to assume that they will continue to be ignored, or worse, discriminated against. It is an unfortunate presumption that can mean the most willing and supportive of workplaces might lose out to some of the best staff because they have failed to explicitly communicate their commitment to inclusivity. For example, in your policies on maternity and paternity leave, make it clear the entitlements that adoptees, surrogates, single parents etc. would have. The legal minimums are set out on the government's own website, but making reference to them in your policies demonstrates a consideration of LGBT+ routes towards having a family.

Getting it right for everyone

I would not yet argue my school has it right for everyone, but we are working hard. It is a long journey and mistakes have inevitably been made. However, it is important not to be afraid to make them. Don't assume ignorance is the same as a lack of tolerance. I have witnessed people with the biggest hearts keeping quiet because they lack the terminology and not acting because they also lack the confidence to do so.

Advice for an LGBT+ inclusive school from Johnpaul McCabe

The lessons learned by focusing on one protected characteristic offer clear pathways to getting it right for others. Inclusion of LGBT+ staff should not be viewed in isolation but be part of a wider push to ensure inclusion for all and getting it right for everyone.

14: How things have changed for the better
Jane Robinson

It seems fitting that the final story in this book is from Jane Robinson, the founder of Courageous Leaders. To conclude our stories, Jane describes the challenges she faced as a teacher during Section 28 and reflects on the way in which teaching is now a much more welcoming profession for those identifying as LGBT.

I was born in 1961 in Lewisham Hospital and spent my first six months in Bromley in Kent. My parents then decided that the countryside was where they should bring up a family and in 1962 they moved to an idyllic house called The Ridge Cottage in Felbridge, West Sussex. There was only The Ridge and two other houses for miles; we were surrounded by fields. My brother was born in 1963 and we grew up together exploring the local woods, playing football in the back garden, and generally setting out in the morning and coming home when we were hungry.

We both attended one of the local comprehensive schools and got decent exam results, despite the laissez-fair attitude of our teachers who in the 70s had unorthodox approaches to teaching to say the least. Our economics teacher threw board rubbers at us and our politics teacher threatened to 'bite us' if we talked.

I had no idea I was a lesbian, as the subject was never really discussed. I once heard my grandmother discussing Billie Jean King with my mum but neither of them knew 'what she did in bed'. I also remember reading *The Rainbow* by D H Lawrence, but the lesbian affair in the book ended sourly and all my friends said it was 'disgusting'.

In 1979 I went to university in Bangor, North Wales and met my first lesbian. Out of curiosity I attended a gay society meeting, but the two other lesbians wore motorbike helmets throughout the meeting and I assumed I couldn't be gay because I didn't have a motorbike!

It wasn't until my third year that I had my first girlfriend. Just prior to that I had a boyfriend and the changeover was very traumatic. I came out to my horrified parents and then ran away to live with my girlfriend in London. I got an office job in Belgrave Square and thought about realising my dream to be a teacher.

I qualified as a secondary English teacher in 1987. My training was in inner-city London schools, but I didn't think about where I would be most suited to work and decided to apply for my first post in a small girls' school in Kent. I was in the process of growing my hair and had borrowed a skirt suit from Next for the interview, and I felt like I was in drag. The school was in beautiful grounds with an affluent catchment area, and I didn't heed the warning signs. The parents were conservative, the staff were predominantly women earning pin money, and few had ever left Kent. The world's progress had largely past them by.

The interview was successful and I thought nothing of having my hair cut neatly in the style of k.d. lang, the androgynous singer and star of the 2010 Winter Olympics Opening Ceremony. I bought a stylish trouser suit and turned up in September, not expecting to cause quite such a stir. On my first day, sitting in the staffroom, I was greeted by one of the many elderly staff. After an exchange of brief pleasantries she moved straight in: 'Are you courting?'

I must have blinked and tried to work out if I'd time travelled back to Victorian England. I remember just shaking my head and thinking I cannot tell this woman in her tweeds that I live with my lesbian lover in Catford. When you're in the closet, certain allies come to your rescue. I soon made friends with a young man from the geography department who was happy for everyone to think we were in a relationship. At Christmas we performed a Kylie Minogue and Jason Donovan duet and the staff were discussing our wedding plans in fine detail. When my ally met his future wife and had to tell me he could no longer be my school boyfriend, I was the subject of so much pity and he was ostracised by those who thought he had done me wrong.

The country was in the grip of HIV and AIDS paranoia and schools were tasked with educating their pupils in the most obscure ways. Leaflets were printed warning of the dire consequences of unprotected sex. Adverts showing tombstones and icebergs played on fear to promote abstinence, and people openly discussed AIDS as the gay plague. As I waited in the staffroom with the head of science to begin our INSET on the subject, she turned to me and sighed deeply. 'I don't know why we're doing this,' she moaned. 'Let's face it, it's only queers that get AIDS and they deserve it.'

Tell me, why oh why did I just stand there and not answer her back? I stood with my mouth open, like a goldfish, and said nothing.

The end of my NQT year was approaching and the school summer ball loomed. It was traditional for staff to attend with their significant other. It soon became clear that, among the staff, anyone without a significant other was considered the saddest person alive. I had a dilemma: I couldn't take Lisa but I also couldn't go alone. My solution was a master-stroke. I would take Lisa's sister's handsome young boyfriend, sufficiently my junior to command respect from the sixth-form pupils. He was a builder and had the most amazing biceps, and I hadn't thought that his skin colour would cause such consternation. The sixth-form pupils were stunned and swooned when they saw him; my sexuality was definitely not in dispute. However, many members of staff stared at me like I had sunk to an all-time low! I hadn't thought that a black boyfriend was almost as shocking as a lesbian lover.

I finished my NQT year still firmly in the closet. In September a new member of staff joined the English department and I found the courage to come out to her as she seemed so friendly. Little did I know that she was telling everyone about my sexuality behind my back. I was called to the head's office and he politely suggested I look elsewhere for a teaching post, telling me 'Your sort simply does not fit in.'

It was with relief that I left Kent and headed back to inner London, where I managed to find a post under a lesbian head of department. I no longer had to be in the closet and when Section 28 became statutory, I was lucky enough to feel no pressure from its negativity. Friends of mine in other schools were terrified and were envious of my free spirit.

It was during this time that I decided to have a baby. My partner and I acquired some sperm from a friend, cycled it home tucked in the top of my shorts, and inseminated it with a home kit bought from a lesbian bookshop. This was quite groundbreaking in those days and I remember all the support I received from my colleagues. I was definitely out of the closet with staff at school, but lacked the courage to be out with pupils. Of course they asked about my son's dad and naturally I lied; sometimes it was difficult to remember exactly what lies I had told.

After a few years teaching part-time, I moved schools. This meant starting again and coming out all over again. Every gay or transgender person knows how hard this can be. It actually went ok and, as I discovered more and more lesbians and allies, I gained in confidence.

One very brave member of staff came out to the pupils and I decided to follow suit. This was only after I had failed a girl in my form. A gay student teacher and myself decided to have a question box for PSHE. This girl put in the anonymous question, 'How do you know if you're gay?' My student teacher and I passed it back and forth to each other, thinking we were being ridiculed. We both refused to answer it. Eventually we put it back in the box. A year later I opened my walk-in cupboard, only to find two girls in my form kissing. I quickly shut the door. When we spoke later, this girl explained how she'd reached out to us about her sexuality. Quickly I told her I was gay too and she cried with relief.

'I never knew I could feel like this and make something of my life,' she said. 'I can't wait to tell my mum that it's going to be ok'.

Can you imagine how guilty I felt? I knew then that it was my duty to be out and proud! That was 20 years ago. I never thought in my wildest dreams that I would now be running a government-funded programme to support LGBT+ teachers in gaining promotion, and also sharing our successes at a number of conferences.

I joined my current multi-academy trust in 2015 and was delighted to find it a safe space. I quickly became a Stonewall training partner and, with encouragement from one of my headteachers, applied for a government grant to support LGBT+ teachers seeking promotion to school leadership roles. With the help of LGBT+ teachers in the trust and the amazing contacts they had, I devised the Courageous Leaders programme. Headteachers in Essex and Harlow contacted me, asking to be mentors. I was put in touch with Catherine Lee from Anglia Ruskin University, and was delighted that she was enthusiastic about researching how LGBT+ teachers felt about their ability to gain promotion.

My home-grown project blossomed with support from so many different people. They were busy leaders who felt so passionately about this subject that they were willing to give up some of their limited time for it. I also found the Department for Education to be amazingly supportive. The days of Section 28 were long gone and members of the School Leadership Unit published blogs about Courageous Leaders, joined us when we spoke at conferences, and visited our face-to-face days. One member of the DfE said she felt moved to tears when she heard teachers on the course talking about how it had given them so much strength to be themselves.

With a teacher recruitment and retention problem and the issues we have around young people's mental health, it's essential we support our excellent LGBT+ teachers and ensure that they continue to feel that they can be themselves in their schools. Gone should be the days when we feel we have to lie to staff, pupils and parents about who we choose to spend our lives with, and gone should be the days when we have to 'borrow' a fake partner for balls and school fetes.

Advice for an LGBT+ inclusive school from Jane Robinson

Acknowledge and celebrate LBGT+ staff anniversaries and other milestones in exactly the way you would those of all other staff members.

Concluding comments: How the Courageous Leaders programme is making a difference
Catherine Lee

At the time of writing, 85% of Courageous Leaders participants have achieved promotion into positions of senior leadership in schools. The success of the Courageous Leaders programme should also be measured, however, in terms of the changes in the behaviour of the teachers once back in their schools. All mention they feel that they grow in confidence as a result of the programme, and several report that they are more relaxed and at ease with their sexual identity both in the classroom and in the staffroom once back at school. For example, Andrew reported feeling a better sense of self-acceptance as a gay teacher, and more able to reconcile his teacher and sexual identities:

'Through the training provided, I feel I am more self-confident and relaxed at school. I feel more settled and accepting of my LGBT status within the teaching profession.' (Andrew)

Fraser, who was promoted to head of school after attending the course, said that Courageous Leaders helped him to be more open with school stakeholders. He recognised that once he learned to relax about his sexual identity, he could be more effective in his role. He said:

It is because of this course that I feel less apprehensive about my personal life. I am more open with staff and children and am now more confident and relaxed at school... I no longer shy away from the topic of 'being gay' or 'gay people' with children and believe it is important that children see the world is made up of a lot of different people.' (Fraser)

As a direct result of the programme, a number of participants have gained the courage to come out as LGBT at school. Others have approached their headteachers and asked to run LGBT equality and diversity training for school staff. Andrew also set up an LGBT society, becoming an out gay role model for his students. He wrote:

'As a result of this course I feel more open and confident at school. I have set up the school's equality and diversity society, and am much more open about my personal life... I have also organised the school's first diversity week and have confidently challenged staff and students who were resistant to taking part' (Andrew).

As a consequence of the programme, participants report feeling and being much more robust about their sexual identities in the workplace. They say they are more likely to challenge homophobic language and, as Andrew describes, are able to challenge colleagues who do not see LGBT inclusion as a priority.

Challenging the attitudes of others is an important leadership trait. School leaders who provide visible and vocal support for institutional change around diversity, and those that have the courage to name specific issues of difference that need to be addressed, play an important role in promoting equality as the responsibility of all stakeholders in the institution. By becoming visible role models in their schools, our Courageous Leaders disrupt the hegemonic heteronormativity in them. Furthermore, the participants achieving positions of leadership are able to increase the visibility of non-heterosexual identities by promoting LGBT inclusive cultures within their school communities.

The visibility of LGBT teachers in leadership roles challenges the heteronormative assumptions underpinning the ways in which leadership is imagined. In mentoring LGBT aspiring leaders to be their authentic selves, and by supporting them to gain roles in which they are more prominent and visible in the school community, the Courageous Leaders programme is beginning a movement which is serving to queer school leadership. Queering school leadership, within the parameters of the participants' fixed LGBT identity labels, is however a paradox of sorts, as the essence of queer is the rejection of identity labels. But what looms large in the consciousness of our Courageous Leaders is an acceptance that changes to the heteronormative cultures in which they work need to be made cautiously and incrementally.

As a result of the Courageous Leaders programme, participants say that their understanding of what it means to be a school leader has improved, with more than half of the participants describing themselves as better leaders as a result of the programme. As Helen writes:

> 'I feel I am now equipped with a far larger and sharpened tool kit to proceed with applications for leadership roles in schools or alternatives.' (Helen)

The feedback from participants shows that the legacy of the Courageous Leaders programme is a renewed and more determined sense of ambition for almost all those involved. Participants that did not gain promotion themselves during their time on the programme gained confidence by seeing people like them apply for and achieve positions of leadership with support from visible LGBT leaders as mentors.

> 'Following this training I recognise more now than ever that I wish to be a leader of learning and development within my school and the wider community.' (Ben)

Similarly, the quote below from Fraser, a gay male participant with three years' teaching experience, captures the benefits of participation for him:

> 'I believe this renewed self-confidence and support from the network of people I met through the programme made me feel

braver and more able to make further leaps up the career ladder. As a direct result of this programme, I had the confidence to pursue my dream of becoming a head of school.' (Fraser)

Final thoughts

The Courageous Leaders programme represents a distinct leadership development experience for LGBT aspiring leaders in schools. The values explored in the programme of inclusion, celebrating diversity, accepting difference, challenging the status quo and social justice are all vital facets of strong, transformative school leadership. However, for LGBT teachers, the day-to-day management of potentially incompatible personal and professional identities through vigilance, concealment, assimilation and acts of pseudo-heterosexuality take a great deal of energy, on top of what is already a very demanding job. The Courageous Leaders programme affords participants the opportunity to set aside the management of their sexual and teacher identities and concentrate fully on their development as authentic leaders. Once each of the participants is supported to find and embody their authentic LGBT leader self, they go on, with LGBT mentor support, to be more successful than they feel they would have been without the support of the programme, and the networks and supportive community it provides.

At the time of writing, Courageous Leaders has worked with a total of 50 LGBT aspiring school leaders over three years. When LGBT leaders become visible within our schools, they disrupt the hegemonic heteronormativity by embodying a distinct type of leadership that challenges the traditional, heterosexual, white, masculine conceptualisations of school leadership that continue to prevail. Few would disagree that in order to flourish educationally, young people need access to diverse role models, committed teachers and authentic school leaders.

There are almost 500,000 full-time teachers in the UK, and 20,000 headteachers (Torrance, 2015). It is commonly recognised that one in ten of the UK population is LGBT and so it is feasible that there are as many as 50,000 LGBT teachers in UK schools. The Courageous Leaders programme has so far been able to support less than 0.01% of this population. At a time when the average length of service for a headteacher in the UK is just three years, Courageous Leaders demonstrates that a specific LGBT leadership programme presents an important vehicle for improving the diversity of teacher leaders, and facilitating school cultures which enable LGBT teachers to be their authentic selves and flourish within the profession.

So what can you do in your school?

Our Courageous Leaders recommend working towards:

- The creation of a safe culture in the school workplace in which heterosexual and cis staff members are encouraged to be allies to LGBT teachers.
- The celebration of LGBT teachers as role models.
- Opportunities for LGBT teacher identities to be acknowledged in the staffroom and the classroom.
- A welcoming school environment for all LGBT members of the school community. Use posters to celebrate LGBT diversity and recognise LGBT family milestones (such as marriage and childbirth) in the same way that heterosexual and cis staff milestones are acknowledged.
- LGBT inclusion policies that are visited regularly and owned by every member of the school community.
- A commitment to showing zero tolerance of homophobic and transphobic language and attitudes by students, parents or any other member of the school community.
- LGBT issues and themes incorporated into the entire school curriculum all the time, not just in LGBT History Month.
- A fully funded regional Courageous Leaders programme in which LGBT aspiring leaders have access to an LGBT leader as a mentor.

REFERENCES

Torrance, H. (2015) 'Blaming the victim: assessment, examinations, and the responsibilisation of students and teachers in neo-liberal governance', *Discourse Studies in the Cultural Politics of Education* 38 (1) pp. 83–96.